MEETING YOUR MIND

MEETING YOUR MIND

Harnessing the World's Greatest Resource

Carol S. Hyman

Applied Mindfulness Training Press

for Applied Mindfulness Training Press
Barnet, Vermont

www.appliedmindfulnesstraining.org

Printed in the United States of America

ISBN: 978-0-578-49982-6

to Patton

Contents

Introduction

So many problems facing the world today arise from the fact that most of us don't know how to work with our minds. Not even two centuries ago, doctors still went from the death bed to the birthing room without washing their hands, and the word germ simply meant to sprout or grow. When it comes to safeguarding the physical body, we view those days as the dark ages.

In the future, if enough people meet their minds and learn to navigate the energetic realm of inner space well enough to pass that wisdom along, our descendants will view these days as the psychological dark ages. It won't particularly help to spend time thinking about thinking; that all too easily just turns into another way of entertaining ourselves. Rather we need a technique with which to explore the inner space of our subjective experience.

Mindfulness helps develop insight—like keen eyes looking inward—that reveals the nature of the tendencies, attitudes, and propensities that are part of our own particular human baggage. Science tells us such conditioned patterns shape our view of the world; yet we tend to believe that our thoughts accurately reflect reality. This doubtful hidden assumption looms large as a cause of confusion.

Human beings are the greatest natural resource on the planet. If it sometimes doesn't seem that way, it's because confusion gives rise to conflicts—in our society, in the larger world, and at times within ourselves. When disagreements and misunderstandings escalate, we may feel frustrated or even hopeless about what will solve our problems. Even if we do have some idea of what might help, we can't imagine how to work with people who think so differently from us.

But it is possible to untangle confusion and work with conflict productively. It starts by working with our own minds. When we practice mindfulness, instead of believing everything we think, we begin to get familiar with our habitual patterns. With practice, we begin to see through the filters they impose to the world beyond, fragmented though it may still appear given the speedy momentum of our minds.

Eventually we discover within us an omnipresent background of awareness that underlies the everchanging content of our busy minds. You could call it the light of awareness. Just as the sun illuminates the objects of the outer world, the light of awareness reveals the patterns within us that color our version of reality, and thus allows us to discern with greater clarity the patterns that exist in the world around us.

Almost fifty years ago, when I began to practice mindfulness meditation, most people thought it was a weird thing to do. Now it's promoted everywhere: as part of the curriculum in business and medical school and countless other trainings; as an essential component in therapies treating everything from eating disorders and addictions to anger management; in the popular media as an antidote to stress and other irritations; as a self-help tool for becoming more of whatever you want to be; and, in some circles, as a method for reaching spiritual heights.

Anything that gets people working with their minds is a positive development in the evolution of humanity. But a common misconception about mindfulness is that the point of it is to stop thinking so much and just be here now. And while you might eventually find that happening if you practice mindfulness diligently, to see that as the goal of meditation is to miss the point. The point of meditation is to develop familiarity with your inner life. How well do you know your own mind? Not what you think, but how you think.

Your eye can't see itself without the aid of some kind of device, like a mirror or camera. Just so, you can't meet your mind simply by thinking about it, because a stream of thoughts is the natural ongoing production of mind. But there is no external device that can show you your mind. What you need is a technique that interrupts the momentum of the thought process so you can recognize the underlying awareness that is free from content. This awake quality is ever-present and open, like the sky. Your steady stream of thoughts and emotions are like the weather.

The technique of mindfulness meditation, in which you practice letting go of thoughts and resting in the present moment, lets you step outside of the habitual stream of consciousness that most people inhabit most of the time. There are good reasons for doing this, reasons that are more fundamental than feeling calmer or becoming more productive.

Three Reasons to Meet Your Mind

1 Because everything you experience is filtered through it and when you don't know how it works, you can't tell how it colors your perception of reality. Mind is the conduit through which experience flows. It is connected at its deepest level to a reservoir of wisdom, compassion, and other resources; through mindfulness you gain access to the wakeful presence that underlies the changing content of your consciousness. Learning to rest in that wakeful presence, you gain confidence in the workability of your own mind.

2 Because exploring and gaining familiarity with the inner space of experience allows you to detect the patterns you are carrying within yourself and, eventually, to see how those patterns affect your experience of the world around you. Contemplating inner and outer patterns shows us the interconnectedness of energies in space that is the nature of reality.

3   Because the insight that arises from your ability to rest in wakeful presence enables you to meet life's uncertainty with resilience and humor, and to face fear directly. Trying to avoid fear jumbles up inner experience and cuts off access to your untapped resources; meeting your mind fearlessly brings clarity that allows you to see how you can best bring benefit into your own life and the lives of others in every moment.

Although the technique of mindfulness practice involves directing your attention to the present moment, the point is not to be constantly aware of only the present. The point is to learn to tell the difference between resting in wakeful presence and being caught up in your thought process. Once you see the contrast between these two conditions, you can begin to untangle the muddle of mixed-up physical sensations, emotional reactions, and conceptual storylines that most of us mistake for reality.

Meditation is the continual act of making friends with yourself. Instead of treating yourself as a project —something that needs fixing—you could adopt an attitude of friendly inquisitiveness toward what you might discover when you begin to explore the inner space of your experience. You could extend to yourself in practice the same generosity you might show a new friend you're interested in cultivating: without judgement, without attempts to manipulate, without impatience for a preconceived result, you could gently investigate what's there.

By learning to direct and sustain attention in this way, you begin to see the habitual patterns that you carry within you. Insight naturally arises about how those patterns influence the way you perceive the world around you, bringing more clarity about the patterns that exist there. As you discern more clearly the nature of the social reality and the natural environment we human beings share, you see the value of helping in whatever ways you can. And without the habitual filters of discursive mind, your newfound clarity lets you see the most skillful ways you might deliver benefit into each moment.

There are so many ways mindfulness practice is good for you, and there is so much supporting research available on the internet, that I'll limit this to a short list. Among the personal benefits you may derive from meeting your mind are increased focus, creativity, resilience, insight, presence, freedom from conditioned reactivity, and confidence.

But Wait, There's More...

It's the ripple effect. As increasing numbers of us meet our minds, the societal benefits will spread like ripples in a pond, enhancing our appreciation of humanity's common nature and giving us a greater perspective on events, each other, and ourselves. Increased awareness of how our minds work will help render us less susceptible to those who would hack our consciousness and mold our reactivity to their own purposes.

And perhaps greatest of all, discovering that our own minds are workable will foster a renewed sense that society as a whole is workable. Instead of throwing up our hands in hopeless exasperation, we will get up from mindfulness practice having met our minds and feeling ready to meet the world's problems with equanimity and resourcefulness.

Because we don't practice mindfulness for its own sake, or even for our own sakes. We practice so we can apply it to the challenges we face. Some of those challenges are personal, arising in relationships, at work, or in our neighborhoods. Some are societal, involving how countries govern themselves and interact with each other. And some, like the environment and potential pandemics, are global, respecting no boundaries.

Our best chance of meeting the challenges we face lies in meeting our own minds individually, first. Then meeting each other respectfully in conversations, we are more likely to be able to be creative in how best to harness the world's greatest resource, the ingenuity and good-heartedness that are inherent in the nature of our species.

This book's three main sections describe three steps in the process of applying mindfulness. The first step, to Direct Attention, gives an overview of and instructions for how to do basic mindfulness practice. Establishing a regular practice, supported by the practice of mindful journaling, is how to begin. Next, the second section, Detect Patterns, is at heart a deconstruction project in which we take ourselves apart contemplatively to see how we work, exploring our conditioned reactivity.

Then we practice creating the space that allows us to choose how we want to respond to whatever we meet in life. And finally, the third section, Deliver Benefit, explores how to activate our inherent compassion and wisdom and harness our share of humanity's resources in the service of making this world a better place.

Interspersed throughout are See for Yourself exercises, instructions in not just basic mindfulness practice but also in other contemplative tools, some Inner Reconnaissance sections that detail my own journey, and suggestions for how to maintain the discipline of meeting your mind. At the end are some helpful appendices, including a glossary and collected exercises.

If you finish reading this book and apply the instructions within it, your life will be changed for the better, and so will the world when you harness its greatest resource.

Meeting Your Mind

Direct Attention

Attention is the currency that human beings have to spend in the marketplace of time; we can use it wisely or squander it. Mindfulness is the ability to direct and sustain your attention on whatever you choose. Until you sit down and try to keep your attention in one place, you may not realize just how discursive your mind is. Discursive means jumping from subject to subject, and it accurately describes the state of the untrained mind.

Paying attention to how we spend our attention takes work. Most of us suffer from flabby mindfulness muscles. Although people have always appreciated the feats of athletes, not until the mid-20th century did we see scientific proof that physical exercise is one of the most important things any of us can do to maintain good health. Now most of us know that training our bodies in some kind of disciplined way means they'll hold up better to carry us through life. Of course, whether we actually do anything about that is another matter.

Now, in the early 21st century, science has demonstrated how valuable mindfulness meditation can be. Meeting your mind in this disciplined way strengthens your mindfulness muscle so that rather than being discursive—or worse, caught in the momentum of all sorts of unsavory tendencies—your mind can serve you well. The untrained mind wastes human resources.

Operating properly, each human being embodies a unique perspective in which sense perceptions, intellect, and intuition deliver information about, and enable us to interact with, our environment. Contemporary education in the West focuses on intellect. As we memorize facts, process information, and maybe, if we're lucky, learn how to think critically, our rational minds get a good workout. But other components of intelligence are generally ignored, which is unfortunate given that science shows that many, if not most, of our decisions get made on an intuitive or physiological level. Then intellect jumps in to explain to ourselves and others why we chose as we did.

We also don't learn much about how to work with our emotions, how to question our perceptions, or how to voluntarily shift our perspective. In short, we don't learn how to work with the space of our inner experience. And yet inner experience colors our world. Although some of us tend to think in images, all of us rely on concepts to help us make sense of our perceptions and experience. However all too often the untrained mind gives rise to a non-stop traffic jam of conceptual thought; the capacity that could be a useful servant becomes a relentless and fickle master.

So it's worth asking some questions. Since we see the world through the window of our minds, how clear is that window? How clouded with preconceptions, assumptions, beliefs, and reactivity is it? And how often do we even bother to ponder these questions?

What We're Missing

When I was a young woman working in a nursing home, one of the most disturbing things—worse than the feebleness of the residents, or the smell, or the fact that even a self-absorbed twenty-four year old couldn't really ignore mortality in that environment—was how many folks told me that they didn't know where their lives had gone.

How could they let that happen? I wondered, with the arrogance of youth. Many years later, I understand. We miss our lives because we don't fully inhabit them. Instead, our days blur together. All too often we're just doing time, imprisoned by expectations, regrets, plans, memories, and constant evaluation of the world around us and our place in it. But something else is going on too, something those nursing home residents were feeling: a deeper wisdom within us that keeps reminding us we're missing something.

We all sense that wisdom from time to time. We know that it's possible to live more fully, wholeheartedly and genuinely than most of us usually manage. That sense is confirmed by occasional fleeting moments of experience; moments that feel like serendipity or grace. Though they occur unexpectedly and without effort, such experiences show us how much life has to offer when we're fully present.

It might happen when you step out of the shower and stand still for a few seconds feeling clean and re-freshed. Or maybe you open the blinds just as the sun-light catches the trees in a certain way that makes you pause. Or your mother's smile transports you back to childhood at the same time as her wrinkles pierce you with the hard fact of impermanence.

It doesn't have to be a pleasant moment. Sometimes a visceral experience like being sick and vomiting or beung in great pain or grief can catapult us into the present moment. The shock of a sudden death can also jolt us into a more vivid world. Whatever the content of such a moment—good or bad, happy or sad—it stops us. We sense what it is to be alive, and profound gratitude arises.

Before we start thinking, "I'm running a little late," before we jump in the car and take off for our next bit of business, before anything else happens, we just stop —captured by the look on a child's face or the sound of the church bells or the taste of honey on toast. For just a moment, there is reality. There it is, the es-sence of life, in that moment, and we know it.

And then we try to hold on to it.

Because such moments feel so alive, we want them to last. When they don't, we struggle to recreate them. But they can't be forced; that fresh immediacy happens spontaneously, when the speediness of our minds and the pressures of our daily agendas fall away, however briefly. The momentum of our inner chatter is interrupted by our full attention to the experience of the moment.

Our Basic Nature

The fact that such pure, direct experience is what we find when our momentum is interrupted is good news for human beings. It tells us that behind the busyness we've come to think of as normal lies a simple wakeful presence. That wakeful presence is our basic nature.

It's basic because we don't have to do anything in order to have it. It is an unconditional and fundamental part of our human inheritance. Although the laws that govern the universe also apply to us, humans like to think that we're special. It's amusing that we named our species homo sapiens. ("Man knows" is what the term literally means, but most people now concede that women know too.) Take *that*, other species! We are the ones who know.

But what is it that we know? What is it that we're capable of knowing? Well, all kinds of *things*, which change from time to time, place to place. But what's deeper than that?

What's deeper is the capacity to know at all. There is a continuity of awareness that knows it is aware inherent in all of us. But we're usually too busy to notice. If someone said, "Stop right now. Listen. I'm going to tell you something very important. You do NOT want to miss this," you would probably put your habits on pause and sit right up.

Then you might notice. That's it. That state right there. You paying attention. You don't want to miss this. It's your life: you don't want to miss it.

Whatever our conditioning, whatever our circumstances, whatever the content of what we know—behind all that is our own wakeful presence, our ability to be aware in the moment with whatever is going on. It's inherent, natural, and unconditional, which is not to say that we don't lose track of it. We do, much of the time, but we needn't. If we explore our human equipment and learn how to use it, we needn't ever have the feeling that we're missing our lives.

Most of us though, if we're really honest with ourselves, would have to admit that sometimes we don't mind missing life. The unpredictability of situations, the absolute certainty of eventual death, the awkwardness of being aware without knowing what to do—remember adolescence?—can make us so uneasy that we long for oblivion, or at least distraction. It takes courage and strength to be awake all the time. A straight shot of life can take your breath away. Sometimes we're not sure we're up to it. We doubt ourselves and that scares us. Then the fact that we're afraid scares us even more. We'd prefer not to notice that, so in an attempt to get comfortable we think about something else.

Inner Reconnaissance:
A Personal Story, Part I

When I was seven years old, bedtime always found me in a state of high anxiety. Now, I realize that there were good reasons for it but then all I knew was that I didn't like the way I felt. I didn't want to go to sleep because I wet the bed most nights and I hated waking up cold and smelly and having to go get my mother. I hated hearing her sigh as she put down a towel so I could sleep till morning when she would once again wash the sheets, and I hated how the grown-ups talked in whispered tones about my problem.

I didn't want to think about all that when I was lying there trying to go to sleep. Luckily for me, in second grade we started learning the multiplication tables. A life raft. The class only went through the threes, but by the end of the year I was up to the tens. Over and over each night I mentally recited my soothing mathematical rosary. The results won me praise at school. After I mastered the twelves, I branched out to other subjects: state capitals, dates of battles, and eventually, as I became more aware of my peers, thorough recaps of who'd said what to me at school that day. Thus I laid the foundation for a lifetime of mental chatter to ward off discomfort, without ever realizing that was what I was doing.

Years later, at an intensive group meditation retreat, this habit became impossible to ignore. About thirty of us had signed on for twenty-eight days of more than nine hours a day sitting silently. We were supposed to be doing basic mindfulness meditation, focusing attention on the breath, but my mind was so full I couldn't corral my attention and bring it back as I'd been instructed. "Relax into it," I remember someone saying. Hah. They might as well have been speaking Swahili.

Too proud to flee in failure, I made myself sit there. Too wound up to come back to my breath, I decided that rather than watching my thoughts race around wildly, I would choose something productive to think about. I would set my mind to a task. I would plan my wedding! Over the weeks of the retreat, harnessing the power of my deep desire to be perfectly hitched, I worked out every detail. Except one. I conveniently overlooked the fact that I didn't have a boyfriend, much less a fiancé.

I wish I could say that at that point I woke up and wondered what I was doing, but it wouldn't exactly be true. It took me a while longer to see how I was maintaining a cocoon of conceptual thinking so I wouldn't have to feel my discomfort.

I'm not the only one. We all create cocoons to buffer ourselves from the starkness of unmitigated reality. Sometimes we need them to ease us, to help compensate for how helpless we feel when we don't know what we can rely on. Our cocoons consist of habitual patterns, spun from threads of biased perception, familiar behavior, emotional reactivity, and relentless conceptual thinking.

We use them to shield ourselves from the fundamental uncertainty of human existence. In the process we miss our lives.

See for Yourself

Maybe it's because I'm a salesman's daughter, but whenever somebody pitches something, I'm skeptical. What exactly are they pushing? Is it something I really need or is it a passing fad? How will I feel about it in a year? Ten? Can I live without it? Seriously, in a world with so many choices, these are questions we should all be asking ourselves.

Awareness is your perception of situations or facts; like a light, it illuminates reality. Attention is the ability to intentionally gather and aim the light of awareness. Depending on whether your attention is focused or scattered, your awareness may be bright and vivid or dim and foggy. In most of us, attention is often divided. We experience awareness as more like a kaleidoscope than a laser beam; we're entertained going around in circles instead of cutting through to what's actually important.

This book is trying to sell you on an idea: that the discipline of paying attention to your inner experience will bring your deepest motivations to light and allow you to deliver maximum benefit into the world. Does that sound like something you need? Do you really want to live an unexamined life? Bring your critical intelligence to this pitch.

As the car salesman says, there's nothing like a test drive to convince you. This little experiment in three parts is likely to prove more convincing than a thousand words of persuasive prose.

1 First, establish a baseline: try to simply be there—wherever you are—in the room, in your body. Pay attention to keeping your attention in the present moment, without thinking of past or future. Do this for a few minutes.

When you stop, take a minute to reflect on your experience.

Was it easy to stay present?

Did you find your mind wandering?

How often did you forget what you were doing?

2 Now look at your hand. Hold it up in front of you and really pay attention to it, appreciating every detail of its physical form—its shape and color, its lines, your nails, how the light hits it and reveals the texture of your skin. If your mind wanders, gently come back to looking at your hand and see if you notice anything new. Keep doing this for a few minutes.

3 Rest for a moment and then look at your hand again. Bring the same focus and clarity to it that you did before. Then, without moving your hand or your gaze, think about what you had for breakfast.

What did you notice about the experience of simply appreciating your hand?

Did it change?

What happened to your perception when you thought about breakfast?

Most people come away from the first part of this exercise amazed at the number of thoughts they have and how unruly and intrusive they can be.

The second part demonstrates that when you really pay attention to something, your perception of it becomes more vivid and direct. Your awareness is focused and the light is bright.

The third shows how, when you think about something else, the fresh immediacy of perception gets clouded over. It's as if you were looking through a filter or fog. Attention is scattered and awareness dims.

Now, take a moment to contemplate the implications of this exercise: Considering how many thoughts you had during the minutes when you simply tried to be present, how much of your life do you think you miss?

Basic Mindfulness Meditation Practice

Walking around in the world while caught in our thoughts, we not only miss out on the vividness of direct perception, we also fail to realize how those thoughts color the way we experience reality. But the purpose of meditation is not to eliminate thought. The ability to think—to use concept to review the past, plan for the future, and imagine things that don't yet exist—gives us enormous creative power. However that power is squandered when discursive and distracted conceptual thoughts seize control of our awareness.

There are numerous types of meditation. The purpose of this particular kind of meditation is to learn to recognize when you are thinking, and to cultivate the ability to bring your attention back to the present moment. Simply noticing the difference between when you are caught up in thinking and when you are fully present strengthens your mindfulness muscle and lets you start choosing how you want to spend your attention.

A Few Tips Before You Begin:

Find a quiet, comfortable place to sit. This could be on a cushion on the floor or in a chair with your feet flat on the ground.

It's a good idea to set a timer. Ten minutes is good to start, although if you can't manage that, even five will begin to help you meet your mind and strengthen your mindfulness muscle.

In this type of meditation, it's good to keep your eyes open, with a slightly downward, soft or unfocused gaze. The reason for this is that we live our lives with our eyes open and meditation is not a retreat from life; keeping your eyes open facilitates mindful transitions between sitting practice and the rest of your day.

1 SIT. Settle into a comfortable position. If you're on a cushion, your legs can be crossed on the floor in front of you. Knees should be below your hips. Sit up straight without being rigid, with a strong back and a soft front. Let your hands settle naturally on your thighs. Don't be afraid to adjust your position as you go. Meditation is not an endurance test.

2 SETTLE. Bring your attention to what it feels like to be sitting in this particular space in this particular body in this particular moment. Allow yourself to feel your weight of your body on the cushion or chair. What do you notice? What physical sensations do you feel? Perhaps there is tension somewhere in your body. You might notice sense perceptions — a nearby sound or the temperature in the room. Whatever you notice, just allow your attention to be on the simple experience of being present in your body right now.

3 ATTENTION ON BREATH. Once you've settled, it's time to bring your attention to a reference point in the present. There are many possible choices but the simplest is your breath, because it's always with you and it's hard to work up too many thoughts about it. See where you notice your breath most clearly in your body. For some people it's in the rising and falling of the chest and abdomen; for others it's in the sensation of the breath as it passes through the nostrils. Wherever it is for you, spend some time simply noticing the breath as you inhale and exhale.

4 DISTRACTION. This isn't actually an instruction, but more an acknowledgement of what's bound to happen. Thoughts will arise and at some point you'll notice that you've forgotten all about your breath. That's fine! That's actually the whole point—learning to notice when we are thinking, and then practicing coming back to our chosen focus.

5 COME BACK! Actually, at the moment you notice that you've been thinking, you're already back in the present. So just redirect your attention to the breath. Continue cycling through steps 3 – 5, coming back to the breath with gentle persistence, until the timer goes off.

Some Reminders:

- It's important to sit for the whole amount of time you've set for yourself. This is also a practice in patience. One image for this process is that it's like trying to feed a toddler with a spoon. Whether you think it's going really well or going really badly, any time you stop and pay attention, you're getting information about you and your patterns.

- Don't get discouraged by distraction. If you were doing a bicep curl and you kept your arm extended the whole time, you wouldn't get much exercise, but keeping it curled up won't do much either. It's the action of moving back and forth, tensing and releasing, that strengthens the muscle. Just so, it's the alternation between being caught in thought and coming back that strengthens the mindfulness muscle.

No Good or Bad Practice

Years ago when I was in my mid-twenties and prone to reckless leaps into the unknown, I decided, with very little experience of meditation practice, to do a solitary retreat deep in the Colorado mountains in the middle of winter. Had I given any consideration to how hard I found spending time alone even at home, and how constantly I sought out companionship of all sorts, I might have realized that lack of meditation experience wasn't the only obstacle I would face.

These days, someone with as little sitting practice as I had at the time would be advised to meditate a lot more, probably with a group, before considering such an endeavor, advice I likely would have gotten back then too had I mentioned several relatively recent psychiatric hospitalizations. But I didn't mention those when I was interviewed by the person responsible for scheduling retreats in the isolated cabins. The idea of solitary retreat had piqued my romantic fancy and I wanted to present myself satisfactorily. I succeeded and was booked for ten days just before Christmas.

On my arrival, a man named Dan helped me carry my backpack and provisions into the cabin. He showed me how to work the woodstove and melt snow for water, instructed me on the location of the nearest outhouse, and told me he would be back to check on me half-way through the retreat. Seconds after he left, I started to cry. I had no idea why, but I couldn't stop. I cried as I unpacked and set up my cushions and kitchen. I cried carrying wood in. And when I finally lit candles and sat down to meditate, I continued crying.

The basic mindfulness instruction involves bringing attention to the breath, over and over, coming back to that as a focal point whenever thoughts and emotions carry you away. But between tears and the torrent of emotional upheaval and storylines running through my head, I couldn't find my breath, much less return to it repeatedly. All I wanted was to escape.

Our biggest obstacles can sometimes be our biggest allies. In this case, pride came to my rescue. I was unwilling to be known as one who had fled retreat, and so I bargained with myself. The shortest solitary retreat I'd heard of anyone doing was a week. I decided to stick it out alone that long, even if I didn't feel like I was really meditating.

Snowstorms and moonlight and coyotes kept me company but weren't much comfort. Still, I persevered. Expecting a visit from Dan on the fifth day, I planned to tell him that I would be leaving early. But he showed up a day late, and so by the time we talked I had already started to pack for departure the next day.

Why? He wanted to know, clearly hoping to convince me to stick it out. Because, I said, I'm a bad meditator. I try to do the technique, but I can't. Yesterday, I told him, I only remembered to come back to my breath three times in a whole day of sitting. He laughed. Then he said, "Well, look at it this way: three times yesterday, you were actually here!"

Surprising myself, I laughed too. And although I did indeed leave the next day, I didn't stop practicing meditation. Now that I had met my mind and seen how wild it was, I was determined not to quit until I had tamed it.

So I speak from experience when I tell people there's no bad meditation. But no matter how many times I say it, people have a hard time believing it. I suspect it's because, like me heading into my cabin, they have a preconceived idea of what meditation should be like: a way to reduce stress and anxiety, a peaceful and serene state, a blissful sanctuary from the chaos of life. Others think the purpose of meditating is to clear our minds of all thought.

But in this type of meditation, what we're undertaking is a form of investigation. And as with any investigation, if you start out with an idea about how it should go, you won't fully see what's going on. You miss clues if you believe you already have the answer.

Asked to describe her experience of practice, a recent workshop participant said, "It was going great for the first three minutes and then…not so great for the last seven." When I asked why, she said the chair was uncomfortable; she got fixated on physical sensations and had a hard time coming back to her breath. Reminding her it's fine to move when uncomfortable, I also said that while the first three minutes were great, the last seven minutes were…also great! They may have even been better. Because we don't learn so much when everything is easy and smooth; we learn about ourselves from challenges—the hard stuff.

That's why I congratulated another participant who reported dejectedly that her practice had gone terribly: her thoughts wandered, but even worse, she said she found coming to the surface, for lack of a better word, "a lot of crap," as well as tears falling. And she'd said to herself, "Shoot! This is supposed to be restful…"

The fact that she used the word "crap" reminded me of something the man I learned meditation from said. It could be paraphrased as "The ground of wakeful presence is fertilized with the manure of experience." All the shit life hands us actually enriches our experience if we know how to work with our minds.

If we don't, we try hard to avoid crap. Discursive thinking is one way we distract ourselves from things that would make us cry. But tears are a sign that we're dipping below the surface and touching something real. We're allowing ourselves to feel the depths of what it is to be human. Human experience is rich, with many aspects. We tend to seek what makes us feel good and avoid what doesn't. That strategy keeps us scrambling and doesn't work in the long run anyway.

Of course, meditation can sometimes be peaceful or quiet, and it's nice when that happens. But thinking of meditation as the continual act of making friends with yourself invites a different perspective. If you met a friend for lunch and she started crying, you wouldn't tell her to stop blubbering because this is supposed to be a nice, peaceful lunch. You'd ask what's wrong. Then, if you were both lucky and open, she might be able to tell you. At the end of the conversation, you probably wouldn't say lunch had gone badly. On the contrary, you'd likely feel more deeply satisfied than if you had spent the time discussing the latest movies you'd seen.

Being present for all of our lives, even the hard parts, is the greatest benefit mindfulness practice brings. Because, try though you might, you can't avoid life's tough stuff. Even if you can temporarily avoid life's obstacles and challenges, you can count on eventually facing some of them, including your own death. The ability to fully inhabit your life even when things are uncomfortable is what mindfulness training is for. It can help you find deep satisfaction in every moment, whether you're bustling down a busy street or crying alone in a cabin.

Meditation practice is so simple you may not think anything at all is happening when you begin. But keep at it and you will notice the fog gradually lifting. It's hard work, exercising your mind. It's something you have to keep plugging away at.

You can always come back. It doesn't mean you won't get distracted again two seconds later. And even if after getting distracted, you don't come back until a half hour, an hour, a day later, it doesn't matter. The more you practice, the more you'll remember to return. A kind of trust develops, a certainty in this space you can always shift into, where you're not judging, you're simply noticing. Simply being. Wakeful presence is always there, for you to return to and rest in. It's a space with great power and real freedom.

Practice Good Mental Hygiene

Think of meditation as mental hygiene; not unlike dental hygiene. You wouldn't leave your house in the morning without brushing your teeth. Once it becomes part of your routine, you'll find taking a few minutes to check in with yourself is just as indispensable when preparing yourself to go out into the world and interact with other people.

Try to Sit at Least 10 Minutes a Day

You can sit for longer if you like, but it's important not to set unrealistic goals, since failing to meet those goals is extremely disheartening. It's helpful to try to sit at the same time every day, so that it becomes a part of your routine.

Keep a Record of Your Practice in a Journal

As soon as your ten minutes are up, write in your journal the date and note how long you sat down and meditated. Then write just a few words that come to mind to describe the experience. It could be as simple as "sleepy" or "agitated." Or you might note "Couldn't stop thinking about work." This is a great tool for beginning to track your patterns and hold yourself accountable.

If you remember something important that you need to do after you get up, you can make a quick note about it so you don't get stuck trying to hold on to the thought. Just jot it down and get back to your practice.

If you miss a day or two, don't beat yourself up. Just come back! And since it's helpful to have an idea of where you are going when you embark on a journey, please continue reading the other sections of this book, which will give you an idea of how cultivating mindfulness and learning to rest in wakeful presence can help you navigate your life more skillfully.

DETECT PATTERNS

WHEN I WAS A CHILD IN THE FIFTIES, A FEELING OF confidence pervaded society. The war had been won and we'd entered a new era. Progress was America's theme song. Polio was no longer a threat, and a cure for cancer looked to be right around the corner. Science was closing in on the mysteries of the universe. Some people were even talking about the mysteries within us; I remember asking my mother what a Freudian slip was. Although the notion of unconscious motivations was puzzling, psychoanalysis offered the promise that even mental problems had solutions. Meanwhile, economic opportunities seemed boundless. The consensus, at least in my family, was that things weren't bad and would only get better, as long as the Russians didn't blow us up.

Or so I remember. But eyewitness reports are notoriously unreliable even when the observer has no agenda. In everyday life, people do have agendas. Plus unconscious influences are at work and, by definition, we don't know what they're up to. So memory generally confirms our current storyline. Nowadays the storyline of the fifties might seem sweetly naïve. Or dangerously arrogant. Or any number of other possibilities, depending on one's storyline.

Stories Versus Reality

Human beings are storytellers. That's how we make sense of our lives and give them meaning. Some stories have attained social consensus, like the idea that the pieces of paper we call money have value, or that individual liberty is one of the highest values to which humans can aspire.

Stories are always an overlay, an interpretation of what is. They enable us to accomplish great things but can also get us in a great deal of trouble if we mistake them for reality. A participant at a recent workshop asked me, "Don't our stories make our reality?" And of course they do, to a large extent; therein lies both the power and the problem. For example, less than two hundred years ago in this country, white slave owners told themselves—citing stories in the bible to back them up—that the people they were enslaving were less than human and divinely designed to be used as unpaid labor.

Someone else asked, with a note of cynicism, "Well, I'm eager to know then, what is reality?" I appreciated the skepticism because there is no real answer to that question. Reality can't be pinned down in words, no matter how fine a story we spin. Attempts to describe it will vary depending on who's talking, but the fact is that reality can only be experienced directly. About all you can say is that reality is things as they are, as opposed to things as we interpret them.

Our interpretations come from our involvement in a story rather than simply being present, observing. It's not that stories are bad, per se, but only by recognizing the stories we tell ourselves as stories will we see how they congeal and shape what we take for reality. And only then can we choose to drop stories that cause harm, giving us a clearer view of things as they are.

Assuming that reality is as it seems to be is what social psychologists call naïve realism. A more nuanced perspective takes into account what science tells us about space and uncertainty. While there's nothing new under the sun, each moment arises fresh and up-to-date in personal experience when we drop our preconceptions and habitual patterns. Resting in wakeful presence, we are vehicles constantly delivering creation into experience. Or experience into creation. Our inner and outer perceptions merge in awareness.

Until we stop weaving the storyline shroud that keeps us cocooned in our limited lives, our situation is as exhausting as an endless ping-pong game. We have to constantly keep checking things out, shuttling back and forth between who we think we are and what we think is going on around us. This continual self-reference saps our energy and distorts and limits our view of the world —a world we could actually be inhabiting fully if we weren't so caught up in what we think about it.

It's a reciprocal process: as the content of our thoughts changes, so do our opinions and, more slowly, our storylines; as storylines and opinions shift, the content of our thought follows suit. And so it goes, and with it go our lives, unless we pay attention and notice how fickle this whole process is, and how it shapes what we call real, and how much we miss because of it. Filtering life through storylines and opinions may be "normal" in the sense that most people do it, but as the exercise in part one shows, when we're caught up in thinking, we don't see as clearly. Our perceptions and commentaries get all jumbled together. We may not even realize that there is anything beyond what we believe and think about things.

For example, one prevailing storyline these days says that we are entitled to our opinions, and many of us do hold them dear. Pundits post them, pollsters sample them, and politicians pay homage to them. Thus they shape public policy. But who bothers to try to find out how well-informed those opinions are?

Now contemplate the nature of opinions: everybody has them, everybody likes their own better than anybody else's, and mostly they're just a lot of hot air. A little like flatulence. While our beliefs are somewhat more, ahem, substantial.

No wonder it can get stuffy in our cocoons. We might long for a breath of fresh air. We might even get tired of hearing ourselves think and, instead of generating confusion, become inquisitive. A penetrating question – like "Who am I right now?" – might arise naturally, and we could actually take time to allow an answer to arise that illuminates our state of mind. Right now I'm a person who can't stop crying. Right now I'm a person who is late for an important meeting. Right now I'm a person who is right, goddamn it. Right now I'm a person who can't be happy unless somebody else changes.

Our Cocoons, Ourselves

We think we know who we are. But what we think is only a small part of the picture. In most of us, our connection to reality is obscured by the constant storylines about experience that we maintain and mistake for things as they are. Comfortable in our own perspective, we're nestled within a cocoon we don't notice because it's pretty much invisible from the inside.

Comprising our deepest beliefs about ourselves and life, storylines provide the ongoing themes that pervade our inner running commentary.

"It's a dog eat dog world."

"No matter what I do, it's never enough."

"The rich get richer."

"I can never get a break."

"The universe always gives you exactly what you need."

"Life is hard and then you die."

Often unconsciously, we adopt certain beliefs and craft them to support and define our experience.

If storylines structure the cocoon, opinions are like the wallpaper and we're constantly redecorating, changing our minds about where we stand on everything from the weather to the best way to boil eggs. Identifying with constantly changing content spun from threads of our present affiliations and fashioned on the loom of history constructed from memories, we prop up our belief in ourselves as solid individuals, separate from other people.

Of course, it's a lot easier to see other people's cocoons. Got a co-worker who won't stop talking? Or a friend who finds the cloud in every silver lining? Maybe you know folks who constantly crack their knuckles, clear their throats, or wiggle their feet? Of course you do. It's harder to see your own cocoon, although we all have our habitual rituals, from what we want when we wake up in the morning—coffee, tea, or the snooze button?—to whether we soap up or shampoo first in the shower.

It's not that habits themselves create problems; often our habits serve us well. The habit of flossing your teeth makes it more likely you'll keep them. Learning to drive a car calls for careful attention to every detail, but once mastered, the necessary skills become habitual and we can merrily, and safely, roll down the road while listening to the radio, talking with a friend, or calculating whether we have enough gas to make it to the next exit.

A habit that serves you is one that you consciously decide to cultivate and use. Such a habit can free you of the need to keep your awareness on a mundane or repetitive task, enabling you to employ your uniquely talented and well-placed human resources more productively. That kind of habit creates more space in your life.

Wisdom comes from space, so that's a good thing. But wisdom can't come into our awareness if we unconsciously fill it with habitual patterns. This is something most of us do most of the time, for a variety of reasons. Sometimes, like me as a little girl reciting times tables, we keep our minds busy so we don't have to feel whatever is lurking beneath our conscious awareness. Sometimes a strategy works to get us what we want and repeating it seems like a good idea, so we keep on wheedling, or fudging the truth, or pitching fits. Sometimes we pick up a pattern from someone else. But although our cocoons, padded as they are with familiar habits, can feel quite cozy, they prevent us from experiencing reality directly: we see the world only through their gauzy filters.

Your cocoon expresses the conditioning that has shaped you, but you don't have to stay stuck in it. All you need to do, to begin to dissolve the cocoon and break your conditioned spell, is to recognize it. You do that by learning to rest in the wakeful presence that does the recognizing. In that way, human nature works in our favor. Before we can leave the cocoon, though, we have to explore it thoroughly; it too is part of our human inheritance.

Unlike Pavlov's salivating dogs, we can ask what's going on. We can exercise our right to curiosity. We can invite an inner voice to keep reminding us, "This is important. Wake up! Pay attention." When we do, when we notice wakeful presence, for a moment we stop spinning the cocoon. We're just awake in space. It's not even that "I, so-and-so, am sitting here awake in space," because that's actually the beginning of a story.

But stories can also tell us something about the nature of reality. So in this case, let me tell a little more of my story.

Inner Reconnaissance:
A Personal Story, Part II

In my own long strange trip, a harrowing birth and early illnesses gave way to childhood and teen years marked by afflictions then termed psychosomatic. "Mommy, I don't feel good," was my constant refrain. There were certainly pleasures—I loved to read, excelled as a student, and ate as much as I wanted without gaining weight—but I also missed months of school with asthma, wet the bed up into my teens, and wasn't much liked by other kids.

Near the end of high school I ran away from home, discovered drugs and sex, and tanked my previously stellar scholastic reputation. Over the next few years I would make the acquaintance of numerous shrinks, see the inside of more than one locked ward, and meet the business end of a stomach pump. I was so desperate that when a psychiatrist recommended shock treatments, I said, "Let's do it," and we did. Jolting voltage tossed all my patterns up in the air for a few months, but when they settled back down I was still in in the grip of a nervous breakdown.

Then one day I came across a book that recommended sitting still and making friends with myself. It sounded like a good idea but I didn't have a clue how to do it, so I decided to look for the book's author. Because I found him and he showed me, I can write today with confidence about how to connect directly with experience.

Chögyam Trungpa Rinpoche, a brilliant and controversial teacher, helped bring to the West wisdom that had been nurtured in Tibet. He began teaching

Buddhism; later he introduced teachings that came to be known as Shambhala Training, translating ancient wisdom into accessible language and bringing a fresh non-sectarian perspective to the western world. I taught this program to groups large and small for more than thirty years, instructing others in how to cultivate mindfulness and awareness so they could connect more directly with their lives.

Little did I know that during all that time my own meditative discipline was serving as a kind of band-aid, helping plaster a reasonably attractive facade over what my storyline labeled "my previous problems." It would take more than half a lifetime, filled with cloudy events that took their own sweet time revealing their silver linings, for me to learn one of life's most basic facts: you don't know what you don't know.

The life you think you're living is only the tip of the iceberg. When memories that had been locked away for almost fifty years finally surfaced, I realized I needed to face my demons. I sidled up to what I'd been running from, learning to embrace boredom, keep company with discomfort, and even endure excruciating pain with intermittent but genuine equanimity. Perhaps hardest of all, I had to figure out how to make friends with uncertainty. This was a journey without map or itinerary, and I had no notion of where it would lead.

I only knew I didn't seem to have a choice. Wisdom was nagging at me. Like deeply buried gold, it was alloyed in the tissues of my body, bonded with the residue of events I hadn't understood when they happened. Excavating those memories and extracting that wisdom has been a long process. As a young child, I asked my mother why people didn't come with instructions. I hoped a user's guide to being human would help answer the kinds of questions I now faced: Who am I, really? What is my place in the world? What is good mental balance? How can I tell if I have it, and what can I do if I don't? What can I do if I don't know, or don't like, the answers to those questions?

Since these questions aren't easy to answer, usually we don't even ask them. In exploring the causes of my often unexpected and sometimes unwelcome behavior, I discovered how complicated "who I am" can be. I spent a lot of time alone, navigating the inner space of experience. In the process, what I started out thinking of as my demons—neurotic tendencies that would take over my life from time to time—came to seem more like passengers. Instead of the discrete individual self I expected to explore, I found that, like Walt Whitman, I contained multitudes.

Some of my passengers were heavily laden with baggage. Some hijacked my life from time to time. Some carried on conversations in my head, while others only lurked until I became quiet. In the beginning I identified with all of them. I called that chatter me. Eventually, though, I came to think of myself as a vehicle, and I learned to manage, through trial and more error than I care to recount, the needs of my competing inner constituencies.

In my own case, it would take over a decade to meet my passengers and unpack their baggage. That's because I'd done a good, solid job of packing discomfort and anxiety away in the cocoon I'd constructed to help me face the world. I'd had to, to survive. But the black box of my subconscious continued to hold all I had pushed away; even after having practiced meditation for many, many years, something in me kept generating—like one of those bubble machines you can rent for parties, only on speed—unpleasant thoughts.

I mean seriously nasty thoughts. I found fault with the world around me all the time. I secretly thought other people were inferior, which didn't stop me from feeling like I constantly needed to prove my own superiority. I never stopped strategizing how to manipulate things to get what I wanted. And then there were contributions from darker places: thoughts that the world would be better off without me in it, or that everybody knew I was a fraud. Each time I looked in the mirror, an inner voice would say, "You're so full of shit."

When I first met Trungpa Rinpoche, I told him my story about mental hospitals and shock treatments, which were still, at that point, fairly recent events. After relating my troubled tale in some detail, I told him that finding his book had probably saved my life and that he should know who I was because I was sticking around.

He listened without a word until I'd finished and then reacted to my oft-told story as no one else ever had. "You must be very smart, sweetheart," he said. Then, "Please sit. Please, please, sit."

Sitting was the hardest thing I had ever done. As soon as I plopped down and stopped keeping busy, my inner demons took over. It was all I could do to stay on my seat. During the retreat in which I planned my imaginary wedding, I never settled down once in twenty-eight days. At tea break one afternoon, the person who'd been timing the previous session and was thus facing the rest of us, came up to me and said, "Did you know that in the last session before tea, you moved 146 times?" If I'd been a little quicker, I might have asked what she was doing in her practice. As it was, I was shocked to realize that my inner turmoil was so easy to see from the outside.

The point I'm trying to make is that I was pretty wild, and if I could do the work of inner reconnaissance, anybody can. The first step is to see what our minds are like, and meditation practice helps with that. But unless we dig deeper, the subconscious bubble machine is likely to keep on putting out thoughts endlessly.

Even after years of practicing meditation and processing recovered memories, I continued to believe that my thoughts reflected something real about me. One that arose regularly was that the world would be better off if I killed myself. Looking at my life—at my two children, who were then teenagers, at my husband, and at my friends—I could see that even with all my foibles, that wasn't true. This world would not be better off if I were dead. So I asked, Where does this unpleasant idea keep coming from? And I dug deeper. Curiosity would, yet again, come to the rescue, introducing me to passengers I hadn't yet met.

But first I had to go through what most people feel when they get a glimpse of how much they've swept under the carpet, shoved in the closet, or locked in a black box: I just wanted to get rid of it. My inner litany went like this: I don't even want to look at this because I can tell you already that this is not who I want to be in this life. This is not who I thought I was. I'm not interested in being a victim, or carrying around old pain. I just want this gone.

After a couple of years of thrashing about, I eventually realized that the only way forward was through—through the mess, through the discomfort, through all that had been rejected. I saw that I had to make friends with all that. I had to be willing to let everything that had been shut away in the dark come into the light of awareness.

I figured out what wise people have always known: no matter how vast our vision might be of where we think we are going, we still have to go one step at a time. One day at a time. Moment by moment. This, now, always. The next breath, the next thought—that's what we have to face.

I didn't know how long it would take to find my way. I didn't know how little I understood about my motivations, my desires, and my own suffering. I didn't know how to help myself or others. And I didn't know what I didn't know.

But reality was on my case, even if I didn't yet know it. It doesn't matter what we think; reality doesn't care. Every moment, reality keeps pushing us to face the full complexity of what it is to be human. If we're smart, we take a good look and see what hand we're playing. Are we playing the hand we've actually got? Or are we playing some imaginary hand?

Of course, sometimes we have to use our imaginations to play our hands.

See for Yourself

Use your imagination and your memory to travel back in time. Think of an event in which you found yourself having a really strong reaction.

Take a moment to clear your mind, then close your eyes and call the situation to mind as vividly as you can.

Can you feel your reaction somewhere in your body? Is your jaw clenched? Is your chest tight? Has your face—or another part of you—gotten hot?

Can you identify an emotional component to it? Are you aware of anger? Sadness? Embarrassment?

Do you remember how you felt about it at the time it happened? Has your perspective on the event changed since then?

What is the story that you tell yourself about what happened? What are the thoughts about it? Do you have any "on the other hand" thoughts or conflicting feelings?

A Vehicle for What?

Six decades of experience, half of it spent helping others learn how to work with their minds, has convinced me that human beings are fundamentally alike. So I now I look at other people as vehicles too. We deliver into this world much more than just our genetic material: we are carriers of cultural norms, bearers of bias and open-heartedness, conveyers of confusion and clarity and more – often without even being aware that we're doing it.

If we pay attention to our inner chatter, after a while we start to recognize certain voices. Sometimes they're regulars and sometimes they're guest stars, but as long as we remain convinced that our thoughts reflect something real about the nature of the solid separate self we assume ourselves to be, we're pretty much at their mercy. Thinking of our inner tendencies as passengers, we can begin to recognize on the spot when an unruly passenger is about to take control of our vehicle.

No metal detectors will stop these hijackers. Our only defense is to identify them instead of identifying with them. As we get to know ourselves better, we begin to recognize our personal weather, the prevailing patterns and the changing conditions. We think of the former as traits and the latter as moods and, if we begin to track our patterns, we start to see which are our most constant companions. Of those, some incline our vehicles to deliver confusion and others to bring benefit. We won't know which are which unless we take attendance.

When our best intentions are held hostage by forces we don't understand, the only way to extricate ourselves is by paying attention. To ransom back our lives, we have to get to know who's on board our vehicles. We do this by spending quiet time looking inward, processing the passenger manifest, so to speak.

The idea of inner parts is not a new one. Freud conceived of the ego, superego, and id. The inner critic and the inner child have gained popularity as useful conceptual tools. Other theories suggest you view your inner parts as members of a family, or as internalized bits of ancestral inheritance, and there are various techniques that promise access to one's different parts.

Most of these strategies are geared toward either exorcising unwholesome parts or integrating all of your parts into your true self. The goal suggested here is neither of those; detecting patterns simply means getting to know what passengers you carry, and how laden with baggage they are.

So Unpack Already

Start with what you think of yourself. Any time you hold a belief that you are someone who always does this or never does that, you miss out on spontaneously discovering that you're bigger than you think. "I could never speak in front of a large group of people." "I have to get to bed by ten o'clock or I'm worthless the next day." "I never leave a task until it's finished."

Such beliefs are like suitcases we carry around, sometimes feeling weighed down, sometimes feeling a sense of comfort in their familiarity. Like nesting suitcases, beliefs often mask deeper beliefs. We may think we could never speak publicly because we can't imagine having anything worth saying or we believe we're inarticulate by nature. Thinking we have to be in bed by a certain time to function stems from believing that our energy is a limited and fragile commodity. Never leaving a task unfinished expresses fear of the messiness and uncertainty of life.

Whatever the sub-text, we pay a real price for all that hidden baggage. Many people labor through life feel heavily burdened, believing we have no choice but to carry our histories and beliefs along with us. Indeed, unless we realize that there is a choice, we don't really have one.

Practicing mindfulness, we learn to recognize patterns going around on the baggage carousel of mind. We can let go of our beloved storylines and beliefs, but first we need to be sure they aren't key to our survival. Therefore, examining the contents of our bags is a valuable, even necessary, process. Meditation practice helps open the latches so we can inquire within.

But Not So Fast

It's worth clarifying the relationship of two of the main metaphors this book uses to describe what we work with when we begin to apply mindfulness. You could think of the cocoon as being made up of different threads of habitual inner sensations, emotions, and thoughts, all so tightly intertwined that you perceive it as relatively solid. As you learn to direct attention and become familiar with inner space, you begin discriminating different recurring qualities; this book calls them passengers. And passengers that took up residence as the result of events you couldn't fully process at the time they occurred tend to carry the heaviest baggage and trigger the most reactivity.

One hurdle to overcome once we start to see the cocoon is the desire to get rid of it all at once, an impulse that only creates more cocoon. Instead of being willing to say, "Oh how nice that I'm getting to know myself. I wonder what I'll discover," we want it to be over. It's like going away for the weekend with somebody we'd like to get to know, and instead of being willing to let things unfold in the fullness of time, we say, "Okay, now I'm going to give you sodium pentothal and you're going to tell me everything about yourself right now."

That would be enough to make anybody run. Our passengers are no different. When we turn inward not because we're curious about what's there, but because we want it get it over with—whatever we think it is, that will make us feel better, or happier, or more fulfilled – we create a constricted environment. It's as if we can't be bothered to make the space in our busy lives to be friendly to ourselves.

If we could love ourselves enough to be willing to be with ourselves being exactly who we are, completely – our lives would change totally. Who else would ever love us that much? You can't pay a therapist to be with you in that way. You can't find a lover who will be with you in that way. You are the *only one* who can do that for yourself. And it takes enormous courage and bravery—real fearlessness, the kind that is willing to face fear head on and feel it—to let go of all our strategies, in order to just be with ourselves, exactly as we are.

It's as if we've been tortured for years by being kept in a very small confined place and not allowed to move. But in this case we're our own torturers; there's nobody out there doing it to us. We've kept ourselves in these small, confined, cramped inner spaces until our faculties have atrophied and our sense of possibility has shrunken.

If we were dealing with a person who had literally been confined, we'd begin to nourish that person very gently. We'd open the space a little, but we wouldn't put them on top of a building, which might freak them out by the contrast. We wouldn't say, "Okay, hurry up! You should be running a marathon next week." We'd say "Strengthen your muscles, stretch a little, everyday feel a little more strength coming back." Eventually that person might run a marathon to a mountain top.

What we are doing in inner reconnaissance is trying to learn how to stop torturing ourselves. There's no need to try to push ourselves out of the cocoon yet; in fact, that's counterproductive. But we could begin to get a little glimpse of possibility that there's a bigger perspective, a sense of workability, and, from time to time, even a little glimpse of calmness.

Patience is our greatest ally in this work. Think about the Grand Canyon. It was shaped by nothing more than drops of water, over eons. Can you imagine, when the first water made its way through that part of the world, the earth saying, "Okay, I want a really big canyon here. How long is this going to take?" Um…no. To do this work, we really do need to cultivate that kind of patience.

Awake In Space

Becoming familiar with your passengers and their baggage tends to undermine the sense of identity associated with the cocoon. You might again find yourself wondering: who am I?

Asking yourself who you are is an exercise that becomes more interesting the more you apply mindfulness. As you begin dropping baggage, that question tends to produce a different answer every time you ask, prompting you to recognize another pattern: who you think you are changes. Sitting down one day, you find you're a person preoccupied with family relationships. The next day, you're a person concerned about money. Another time, you may be a person who just can't sit still.

So it goes, until eventually you begin to realize that there is only one thing you can always count on: the awareness that sees it all. Who I am is someone who is awake and paying attention. Everything else is subject to change.

The fact that we can't pin ourselves down is both liberating and frightening. We're free of being stuck with a fixed sense of self, but without our habitual reference points we may feel shaky. It takes courage to be willing to let go of our fixed beliefs and be open to not knowing who we are. But if we keep at it, we discover strength in that continuity of awareness, and in the flexibility it perceives.

The good news is that we gain an almost immediate reward for being willing to live with that kind of uncertainty: perspective and clarity. As we wade through all our stuff, meeting our passengers and taking note of their baggage, we begin to feel lighter, more spacious. A natural buoyancy, the strength of resilience, begins to manifest. Our sense of feeling harried, hurried, and hassled falls away and cheerfulness, the unfabricated expression of our inherent vitality, rises to the surface.

As we come to appreciate being grounded in our bodies every moment, clouds of complaint evaporate. Then, instead of watching our mental baggage circling on the carousel of time, we may find our minds in each moment as open as the clear blue sky.

Recognize Any of Your Passengers?

DEFENSIVE DAVID, who's always responding to criticism with an attack or excuse. *That's not my fault! If you'd have told me a little sooner I would have had it ready, but...*

BOASTFUL BETTY, who's always talking about her accomplishments and painting herself as a hero. *I knew nobody else was going to do it, so I worked late.*

Pre-emptive Peter, who's always pointing out his own faults before anyone else can. *I'm so stupid. I'm so awkward.*

Worrying Wendy, who's always thinking of everything that could go wrong in the hopes of avoiding anything ever going wrong. *What if no one shows up? What if there's a drunk driver on the road when we leave the party?*

FOMO Frida, who's always fearful of missing out or deliberately being left out. *I wish I had been there. Why didn't they invite me?*

Self-conscious Steve, who's always convinced everyone is watching and judging him. *They're looking at the pimple on my chin. They think it's rude I didn't bring a gift. When they said some people are so oblivious, were they hinting about me?*

Procrastinating Polly, who's always putting things off. *I'll deal with it tomorrow. I don't have time right now.*

Enabling Evan, who's always excusing other people's negative behavior and to avoid conflict. *That's ok, I know you didn't mean it. No worries! It wasn't really that big of a deal.*

Critical Cathy, who's always pointing out other people's flaws and trying to take them down a peg. *She never remembers anything I tell her. He's always late. You really don't get it.*

Untangling Ourselves

If we want to learn to see reality clearly, we have a deconstruction project ahead of us. Our physical sensations, emotions, and thoughts are in a constant process of reciprocal feedback. By virtue of the simple fact that we have bodies, we're agents of action in the world. We have no choice: each moment calls for us to do something—even if we sit and do nothing. Which raises the question of motivation. Why do we do what we do? Why some things and not others? Why *not* things we swore to ourselves we would do, and *why* things we swore we wouldn't?

Part of the answer lies in conditioning. But that's not the whole answer. Most of us, if challenged to explain why we behave as we do, will blurt out the first rationale that comes to mind. Scientists doing what are known as split-brain experiments have shown that people will make up and believe explanations for their actions, even when the reasons they come up with have nothing to do with what prompted the behavior.[1]

Other experimenters, watching brain scans of people who've been instructed to push a button with the hand of their choice, can tell which hand will be used.[2]

---

1 Michael Gazzaniga. "The Believing Brain," excerpt from *The Ethical Brain*. Dana Press, 2005. www.press.uchicago.edu/Misc/Chicago/1932594019.html

2 Brandon Keim. "Brain Scanners Can See Your Decisions before You Make Them," *Wired*. April 13, 2008. www.wired.com/2008/04/mind-decision/

This wouldn't be particularly remarkable if not for the fact that scientists can make accurate predictions seconds (an eternity in neurological time) before the people themselves think they decide which hand they'll use.

Data like this could be disturbing if we really pondered it. It might undermine our belief in ourselves as autonomous agents possessing free will and make us wonder just who we are and why we do what we do. Lacking any way to answer those questions, even the most introspective of us might, after frustrated head-scratching, resort to a seemingly incontrovertible defensive strategy: "That's just who I am."

That was my fallback position for years. But who am I? Okay, at this point I'd say I'm Carol Hyman, a sixty-something-year-old white woman who lives most of the year in northern Vermont. Of course, those things haven't always been the case, so that doesn't define me. I'm a recent widow, mother of two grown children, a writer and teacher, project manager and intermittent recluse, currently in possession of all of my limbs and most of my faculties. But those things haven't always been true either, except for the limbs. So what's constant?

Certainly not my name. I couldn't wait to change it when I got married. Names are a part of our identity; we tend to bond with them pretty tightly, don't like to hear them bandied about, and can get offended if somebody else calls us by the wrong one. Still, since we can change our names and still feel like ourselves, you can't say that names define us.

How about the body, then? That tempting and seemingly obvious answer is, on analysis, unsatisfying. After all, scientists tell us that every cell in our bodies is replaced repeatedly, some faster than others; not one of today's was there a decade ago. If I lose parts of my body, am I still me? So long, limbs! Adios, organs! That's me myself here, waving goodbye.

And what is the sense of identity that travels through dreamscapes, leaving body snoring softly behind? Or the one that people describe as leaving their bodies in near death or out of body experiences? Is that who I am, and is that the self or is that the soul? Is the self the soul? And how in the world could we possibly confirm the answer to that?

Any straw man we set up, we can knock down. No one has ever found any definitive self apart from our personal sense of continuity and our inference, based on observation, that others also continue. (Until they don't.) Logic would seem to demand that if there's continuity, there must be some *thing* that continues, and so even though we can't prove the existence of the self, we be-lieve in it unquestioningly. It seems too obvious to bother thinking about.

If we pay close enough attention though, we come to realize that our substantial sense of me, myself, and I is nothing more than the ongoing entanglement of com-mon threads: body buzzing with tension, subconscious firing fusillades of emotional reaction, and conceptual mind blowing a smokescreen of discursive justification. And the whole thing is not so substantial after all, which is why we have to keep constantly spinning. And which is also why we can stop.

Because we've never learned to interrupt the momentum of our minds, we've gotten all tangled up, like the contents at the bottom of a sewing basket that hasn't been tended in eons. We have to begin to untangle ourselves, sorting out what we've got. We may like what we discover or we may not, but if we aren't curious enough to check it out, we'll travel through life on conditioned autopilot, never learning how to use all our faculties.

That would be a real waste of human resources.

Release Instead Of Repress

If our psyches really were like a sewing basket, they wouldn't be that hard to deal with. You could just dump everything out, sort and save what's useful and throw the rest away. But things are more complicated when it comes to untangling our habitual patterns: at first we're working in the dark, it's hard to tell what's useful, and it's impossible to throw anything away.

Not that we don't try. I can testify to the power of repression as a compensatory mechanism when life is more than we can handle. While not everyone's story is as dramatic as mine, all of us have impulses and thoughts we'd prefer to keep hidden, even from ourselves. Sometimes we succeed. But that doesn't make those tendencies dissolve. Quite the contrary. They actually gain power from the pressure of repression. Coal can be easily burned up, but try destroying a diamond.

When keeping our unwanted tendencies under wraps becomes too difficult, we generally project them out onto other people. What begins as a kind of self-loathing moves from the inner arena to the larger stage of human interactions, where the problem is always the other guy. But everybody is somebody's other guy. And tendencies unattended are every bit as tenacious as germs; like a plague, they spread throughout the species gaining momentum as we retreat into defensiveness. It takes persistence to do this work because our defensive habits are deeply ingrained and we tend to hunker down whenever we feel threatened.

If we pay enough attention to our bunker mentality, we start to see how it's woven; the warp is made by toggling back and forth between subject and object, the weft by switching between rehashing and rehearsing. Finding ourselves distracted, we're too lazy to interrupt distraction's momentum and then we solidify the process, appointing our so-called self the most important kid on the block.

So what happens if those unwanted parts are not pushed down? What if we were to bring our feared and fearful tendencies into the light of awareness? What if, instead of being propelled by the force of our desire to avoid discomfort, we face what scares us or otherwise makes us want to shy away, allowing ourselves to feel all of it without acting on any of it?

The answer, I found out, is that loads are lightened. Not only do we feel better, but people are spared the suffering that would result from those repressed tendencies erupting into the world around us as aggression, which they are so prone to do.

Such bravery and discipline brings a kind of ordinary magic. Instead of lead into gold, inner exploration triggers an alchemy that transforms psychic sludge into clarity and insight, releasing energy that was trapped within the avoided pattern as well as the greater energy tied up in keeping those tendencies pushed out of awareness or projected onto others. So much energy, freed up for more peaceful purposes!

The Space to Choose

Viktor Frankl survived the Holocaust and was a great student of human nature and teacher of how to live a meaningful life. A quote that has been attributed to him delivers this simple but profound insight: "Between the stimulus and the response, there is a space. In that space is our power to choose our response. In our response lies our growth and our freedom."

Here's how it unfolds in daily life. Some event occurs (your alarm goes off; the phone rings and it's a family member you haven't spoken to in years; a coworker asks if you can take on one of their tasks). You appraise the event—does it require action, or can it be ignored? If it does require action, what sort? And then you either do something or don't. This may sound overly simple, but each of these three steps occurs hundreds of times a day. And it's in the juncture between storyline and action that we first can interrupt our conditioned momentum and choose to respond in ways that will improve our lives and the world.

Untangling the threads of our experience to discern the patterns we keep repeating and notice which tendencies habitually occupy our awareness, we start to see more clearly why we act as we do. Our motivations actually arise from some of our deepest inherent wishes: to survive, procreate and experience pleasure; to feel a sense of connection; and to understand experience and find meaning in it. But these desires, which spring from innate wisdom, become distorted when filtered through the cocoon.

For example, our bodies, which bring us information about the world around us through our sense perceptions, also bring us pleasure and pain. In addition, you could say they carry reminders: of every glove that's laid us down, every time we've sucked it up, every cringe or twinge we tried not to notice. Those traces, embedded in the cells of our bodies, may feel tight or sore or numb; they create pockets of tension wherein our subconscious mind's moods can gather like fog in a valley.

The subconscious mind, which is connected to the energetic field underlying the physical world, is the bearer of intuition and ways of knowing that are beyond analysis. At the same time, it attracts from that energetic field tendencies that reinforce the passengers already inhabiting our inner environment. Especially susceptible to occupation are vacuums created when we split off, dissociating from our experience, or morasses when we obsessively stew in our habits.

Conscious mind, when we are paying attention, has the ability to rest in wakeful presence and also to discriminate and exercise our conceptual muscles when needed. Unfortunately, in most of us this mind stays constantly revved up, moderating or distracting us from all this activity; thus conceptual mind loses its clarity in a shit storm of thinking.

This all happens mostly without our noticing. These forces create constellations of habitual patterns that in previous days might have been called demons; in our day we're more likely to label them neuroses or addictions. It doesn't matter what we call them. The way we loosen their grip is by attending to them. We take attendance and pay attention.

Old coping mechanisms want to be seen for what they are,and appreciated for their services; then the fear behind them shows its face and, in the light of awareness, relaxes. We see this principle at work in conflict resolution. The intensity of disagreements tends to diminish, even when there is no resolution, simply because all parties feel that they have been heard.

And so we need to listen to our passengers. Many of us are cauldrons of inner conflict, and the way to resolve it is to invite our attention to focus the light of awareness within, to come aboard and find out who the players are. In inner reconnaissance we sit inquisitively and as we bring our attention to sensations in our bodies, we begin to notice voices and images emerging. Some are familiar. Some may surprise us. We give them all a simple acknowledgement: "Hello, who are you?" or "Oh, hi, it's you again."

The "you" may be the voice that blames everything on somebody else, or that tells you the world would be better off without you, or that crows about what a big deal you are. It may be an image of your face as a young child, or a dark closet, or a bank of cumulus clouds. It doesn't matter what the content may be. Everybody who is on board is entitled to be there, and every image offers information. We just want to know who and what we've got.

To begin an inner reconnaissance project of your own, starting by teasing apart the threads of your tangled yet solid sense of self. You need to explore how your body's sensations, your emotions, and your thoughts combine to contribute to habitual reactivity. Once you begin to discern the components, you can choose how to respond to situations.

We find that space—the gap in which our freedom lies—by paying attention to how our component elements interact. Physical sensations, emotions, and thinking move together so quickly that our experience can feel quite solid. In order to interrupt the momentum of our conditioning, we have to create some space, to engineer a gap. Actually, we don't engineer it because the gap is always there, we just don't notice it when we're full speed ahead. What we need to do is to pay attention to the difference between those three experiential components: physical sensations, emotions, and thinking (see figure on page 72).

Let's say someone does something that makes you mad. First something happens in your body, although you may not notice it there. We tend to notice the emotion first, even if we can't name it; some kind of feeling arises. Feeling is a word that encompasses both physical sensations (I feel sick) and emotions (I feel happy). Emotions have physical components (I'm angry and my heart is racing), while bodily sensations can contribute to emotions (I'm grouchy because I didn't get enough sleep).

Sensations and emotions tend to trigger thoughts which readily morph into stories. The astute reader might

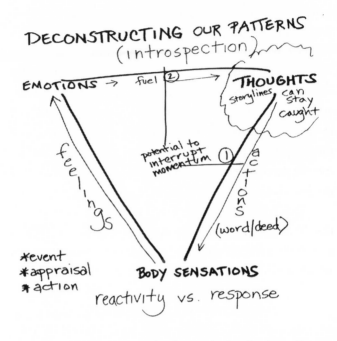

DECONSTRUCTING OUR PATTERNS
(introspection)

EMOTIONS → fuel ② → THOUGHTS
storylines, can stay caught

feelings

potential to interrupt momentum ①

actions

(word/deed)

*event
*appraisal
*action

BODY SENSATIONS

reactivity vs. response

observe in the last example above, the beginning of a story that could spin out into full-fledged self-justification: I didn't get enough sleep because you kept me awake and so I'm justified in being grouchy with you! When our thoughts carry us along to action, which involves using our bodies, we see how energy moves in both directions around the triangle.

The first way to interrupt the momentum of this process is to notice when a thought pattern makes you want to act. Say you get an email from someone that makes you think they're clueless. You might feel irritation and begin planning what to say to point out their inadequate understanding. Your thoughts could coalesce into a story so compelling that your hand starts reaching for the phone to let them know what you think. That's when mindfulness training displays its value: you might stop and ask yourself, will this really help?

As you become more adept in discovering this kind of space and recognizing the gap, you'll be able to intervene between the emotion and the thought. You'll start to identify emotions, seeing how you feel it first, and then grasp for a story to attach to it although often the thoughts and stories have little or nothing to do with why the emotion arose.

With further training, you'll learn how to stay with the direct experience of the emotion as it arises, dwells, and fades away in your body, allowing you to skip the storyline altogether.

Basic Inner Space Exploration

Even though science tells us that our physical bodies are made of atoms forged in star furnaces and recycled endlessly, we still feel like they are us. Now contemplate our character traits, emotions, dreams, and proclivities. Where do they come from and where do they go? Why do some people change and grow while others get stuck going nowhere or head straight to hell on earth? What are those things we call moods, anyway? If we posited all these to be recycled tendencies to which we have a temporary susceptibility, might that change how we work with them?

Deliberate investigation can help us understand the nature of the inner processes that shape our lives. Only through open inquisitiveness will we, like Lewis and Clark, gain access to the intelligence native to that territory.

1   Begin with basic mindfulness practice until you feel somewhat settled. Then close your eyes and bring your awareness into your body.

2   What do you notice? Physical sensations like your weight on the chair or cushion, or the temperature of the air? Sounds or other phenomena delivered through your sense perceptions without any effort on your part? Tightness or pain in any part of your body?

3   Try dropping a little more deeply into your body, letting the light of awareness move like a spotlight throughout your interior. Remembering that your body is energy that has temporarily coalesced in space, pay attention to how energy feels within you – where it flows and where it's stuck. Perhaps several different parts of your body feel connected in some way, even if you can't tell how. Just notice what's there to be noticed. If you can't feel some parts of your body from the inside, that's useful intelligence too.

4   See if a particular area in your body wants your attention during this period of time; if nothing

especially catches your attention, pick an area that you can feel. Now ask an inner question: what wisdom or pain is this sensation holding? Don't grasp for an answer but just allow space for insight to arise. If the idea of passengers resonates with you, try this question: who is on board that wants the spotlight today?

Again, wait. Patience is key.

Once you get the hang of exploring inner space, there are techniques that can help you clear the baggage that passengers carry, which liberates energy trapped in compensatory and habitual tendencies. But the first thing you need to do is to get a sense of the constellation of energetic inclinations and propensities that form your inner firmament.

When you tell yourself a story about how someone was wrong to do what they did and how you're right to be angry, you get caught carrying that around. If you do that enough, you'll carry anger around with you for your whole life, dragging baggage from one situation to another, trailing clouds of emotional residue that you've created storylines about.

But it's not necessary to live our lives that way. We can live mindfully, with wakeful presence from moment to moment engaging openly with whatever arises. But in order to do that, we have to break out of our conditioned responses. We need to learn to interrupt the momentum that creates that reactivity and that baggage.

So when you find yourself solidly behind a story, ask yourself, How do I know that?

Here it gets tricky. You can't necessarily trust your first thoughts in response to that question. Chances are they'll be part of your storyline, a product of conceptual mind blowing off steam. You have to stop, tune in to your basic nature, and access the intelligence underlying the stories. You have to recognize that how you know *is* who you are. You have to be willing to pledge allegiance to your wakefulness.

Basic Contemplation Practice

The purpose of contemplation practice is to harness the power of the conceptual mind. We all have wisdom within that we normally don't have access to because our minds stay so busy—thinking about work, or a conversation we had last week, or what we had for breakfast; there's no space for wisdom to arise.

This Practice Is Useful in Many Situations:

- When something's bothering us and we don't know what it is
- When we have a situation that we're not sure what to do about
- When we want to clarify our goals
- When we would like to bring more clarity and insight into the process of making a decision or understanding an experience

Ideally you would find a quiet place to do this practice and have at least ten or fifteen uninterrupted minutes; that's creating physical and temporal space. As for creating mental space to allow insight to arise, these are the steps:

1   Clear a space with basic mindfulness practice.

2   Bring to mind a question or an issue. Ask yourself what would be helpful to know.

3   Be patient and inquisitive without an agenda.

4   Set aside the first answer that comes up.

5   Go back and see if you can go a little deeper. Ask yourself if there's anything further that it would be helpful to know.

One of the biggest obstacles to insight arising is our impatience to have an answer. Don't struggle for it, let it come to you. If you create space, insight can arise.

Here's an example from my own experience. Once I was having difficulty with a person and the more I thought about it, the more it bugged me. More than bugged me—angry thunderclouds were gathering in my inner weather.

I was on the verge of picking up the phone to let that person know what I was thinking. Luckily, I had enough self-awareness to recognize the stormy momentum and realize that calling at that moment might not be the best course of action. Instead I did this contemplation practice.

The question I asked myself was, "What is the most skillful way to deal with this person?"

The first thought that arose was, "You need to stand your ground." That was interesting, because it did feel like there was a boundary issue.

But I set that aside and thought, "Okay, but is there anything a little bit deeper than that?" And after a few moments the thought that came into my mind was, "You need to see that person's fear." Now a part of me already knew that a lot of what was going on between us resulted from fear, but in contemplation I realized that I was taking personally actions arising out of the other person's fear.

I set that insight aside, and asked myself again what the most skillful way to deal with the person was. And what finally arose was, "Find out what that person wants from you."

So though I started from a place in which I couldn't wait to give the person a piece of my mind, contemplatio led to progressively deeper insights, and the realization that this person had fear that I could actually relate with, and that I could afford to be inquisitive about what was going on between us and what the person might want from me.

Who I Am Is Awake

Although people think of mindfulness as being present in the moment, it doesn't mean trying to hold onto the changing, conditioned contents of each moment. Instead, the fundamental shift that will help benefit all of us will come from some of us transferring our allegiance from the content of our cocoons to the light of awareness that shines steadily behind all the changing conditions.. Then we have to rest there. For as long as we do. And then do it again.

This practice is simple but slippery. It's simple because there's nothing more basic: wakeful presence is always with us whether we notice it or not. We don't have to cook it up, make it better, or hold on to it. In fact, we can't do any of those things, because it's unconditional, our inheritance from the heart of the universe. It's slippery because our most deeply entrenched habit is to identify ourselves with changing conditions. Especially the ones we call I, me, or mine. We take them personally.

But by training to shift our sense of identification, our loyalty shifts to our capacity for being conscious of present circumstances and cargo, and we can't help rediscovering our basic nature, wakeful presence. Eventually we come to see how trustworthy it is, and how good it feels to rest in it. The more we rest in wakeful presence, the less interest we have in joining the war of words—or any other war, for that matter.

The perspective of wakeful presence lets us see how unnecessary all that storm and stress is and how natural it could be for human society to foster cooperation and compassion instead of confusion and conflict. We see that it all depends on us and how well we know—and know how to work with—our minds.

First we take ourselves apart to see that underneath what changes is an awake core that is always within us, an ongoing and unchanging awareness that perceives our ever-shifting conditions. Then we learn to rest in it. Grounded in this awareness, which is our fundamental human nature, we find ballast to hold steady on the journey of life.

Further Tools for Exploring Inner Space

Make a Passenger Manifest

Use your journal to keep a running list of things you repeatedly tell yourself. See if you can identify passengers engaging each other in inner conversations.

Diagram a Thought

Did you ever have a strict grammarian English teacher who made you diagram a sentence? It's at first a some what frustrating and even mind-bending task. But it can offer a valuable lesson: that by examining the function of even the tiniest of words we can see how they hold our storylines together.

When you notice a thought that's not letting you go, maybe it keeps coming up during your sitting practice, or even interrupts your day, set aside some time to sit with it. Give it your attention. Notice what bodily sensations, emotions, and storylines are wrapped up in it. Write about it in your journal. Ask yourself: What other thoughts, emotions, and sensations is it connected to? What's holding it together? You might be surprised.

These and other contemplative practices recommended in this book begin with the ability to direct and sustain your attention so that you can explore from the ground of wakeful presence. Gentleness is always appropriate, so when your mind wanders during an exercise, simply come back to the intended object of your attention.

DELIVER BENEFIT

SEVERAL YEARS AGO, WHEN TWO CHILDREN PLAYING IN the Florida surf were caught in a riptide and swept out to sea, four family members rushed in to rescue them. They got into trouble too. Next four strangers on the beach tried to assist and then there were ten. Ten heads, bobbing in the waves a hundred yards offshore, swimming straight, swimming sideways, bodies floundering. The police were called. They decided the safest course was to wait for a rescue boat.

Others on the shore realized it might arrive too late. Who knows how bright ideas arise in the minds of human beings? Somebody said, "I'm a good swimmer. If I can get close enough, I can pass them along!" Somebody else said, "Form a chain!" and five people joined hands and waded out. Others followed. Soon eighty human beings were linked with one goal, and all ten were brought safely to shore.

News that heartening is rare. Most mornings, if it isn't nature raising a ruckus with hurricanes, earthquakes, fires and the like, it's human beings acting out bad ideas like genocide, mass murder, or even just name-calling in high places. Cry me an on-going oy vey chorus.

But sometimes even mainstream media—which seems to aspire to keep us in a perpetual state of high dudgeon—can't ignore good news. And social media, the platform of the people, in addition to being a platform for spewing bile, helps spread encouraging news. These days it's worth contemplating stories that confirm the fundamental decency of the human race.

If hurricane season always brings riptides, it also brings opportunities for altruism. People of all ages, races, and social classes reach out to help each other in times of crisis. Another human chain formed in waist high water in Houston to deliver a laboring woman to a dump truck that drove her to a hospital where her baby was born. Yes, people can be wonderful. We know that.

So why don't the generosity and creativity that emergency situations call forth deal more effectively with systemic problems we face? I think the answer is that we don't know what to do. When it's clear how to help, most of us are willing to pitch in, in profound life and death situations—the kind that make the news—and in more ordinary ones like reaching the top shelf at the grocery store for someone shorter, or loaning a neighbor a tool, or slowing to allow a driver stuck in the wrong lane to merge.

But how about bigger and more nebulous questions? Why do so many young people turn to drugs, or suicide? What can we do about the bigotry and contempt that some people, including ourselves, may feel for those who are different? How might we balance the world's economies and its environment to sustain good human societies? It's hard to tell what actions will successfully address such problems, and their magnitude can leave us feeling helpless.

That's because of a more fundamental problem: we don't know what we don't know, and what we don't know about ourselves causes a world of hurt. The inner lives of human beings are a mystery, often even to ourselves. While it's relatively easy to see when people's bodies are in danger of drowning, it's trickier to tell when minds are caught in malevolent currents – and people drown there too, every day.

If we want to help them, we have to work with our own minds first. Those people on the beach couldn't have formed a human chain if their hands were full of beach chairs, boogie boards, and beer cans. Similarly, we won't be able to bring benefit into this world on the deepest level if our own inner lives are full of prejudices, fixed ideas, and unexplored baggage.

Everything that arises in our hearts and minds springs from an underlying energy field where tendencies of all sorts reside: polarities like positive and negative, surges of hope and fear, vast reservoirs of wisdom and ignorance. Just as the ocean is the source of all life on earth, this unseen energetic ground gives rise to consciousness and everything it allows us to experience. If we don't even know that this energetic substrate exists, we can't know that we're all connected on that level, nor can we deliver the benefits that come from learning to ride its waves.

Within that energetic ocean, riptides of confusion carry away countless human beings. Most of them believe, as many of us do, that our thoughts accurately represent reality. We believe that there's some inherent part of us—some self—that needs to be defended, and that most of the world's problems could be solved if only other people would just change.

Of course, they will, at some point. And so will we. Change is inevitable; it's also unpredictable and often out of our control. But even if we can't change our circumstances, we can learn to choose how we respond to them.

One way to stop reacting immediately and habitually to everything life throws at us is to cultivate inner space. That space allows us to transcend conditioning and choose how to respond to events. It also brings insight about the nature of the self we've taken for granted, insight that lets us relax the struggle to maintain that self. Then we can choose to manifest courage, resourcefulness, and compassion rather than defensiveness and aggression, and so bring benefit instead of contention.

Before we explore how we can benefit the world, let's look a little more closely at the changes mindfuness may already be bringing about in your own life.

Personal Benefits

The more familiar we get with our minds, the more benefit we derive from our ability to direct and sustain our attention as we choose and detect the patterns within and around us. Mindfulness truly does deliver an inner advantage, enhancing abilities in areas including but not limited to:

Focus

Your ability to direct your attention becomes more reliable and flexible so that not only is it easier to maintain your attention on the task, situation, or entertainment at hand, but also you gain the ability to widen your awareness to take in a more panoramic perspective. And perhaps more importantly given the many interruptions that arise in the course of a day, mindfulness helps you regain focus more quickly after distractions.

Creativity

Rather than being something to strive for, creativity arises spontaneously from the space of wakeful presence and the courage to go beyond familiar patterns. Mindfulness interrupts mental momentum and helps ventilate your mind; fresh ideas can emerge as you think outside habitual boxes and make previously unseen connections. Whether you are whipping up a delicious meal, planning a seminar, structuring a financial transaction, performing a piece of music, or dealing with a difficult work situation, resting in the space of presence allows creative insight to express itself.

Resilience

When you are faced with disturbing situations, familiarity with your own patterns lets you recognize when you are stuck, so you can touch in to a sense of wakeful presence. This makes it easier to maintain emotional balance and move into the next moment less encumbered by your history. You discover a kind of equanimity and are able to recover more easily from trauma, or even just from daily life.

Clarity

Becoming more aware of the patterns of your ongoing stream of thoughts and emotions, and seeing how fickle they are, you begin to recognize more quickly the activity of spinning a story to suit your biases. This insight offers the possibility of taking a bigger perspective, one that allows you to see reality more clearly, discerning what will truly bring benefit as opposed to what may just feel good.

Confidence

The more you come to trust your ability to rest in wakeful presence, the less you feel the need to strategize and defend anything. You begin to feel that whatever happens, you will be able to tap into your inner resources and meet life wholeheartedly.

Societal Benefits

How can we come together? Can we come together? Can we coexist with people who think very differently? We won't progress as a species by focusing on what divides us, whether it's by race, gender, nationality, political perspective, or the color of our eyes. When we're caught up in solid opinions, fearful for the future, and feeling we have to do something, anything, to right the wrongs we see around us, humans have a tendency to look for someone else to blame. Things would be better if only that person, or those people, would just… fill in the blank.

Meanwhile, our blame-ees, who are likely to be just as convinced as we are that their own perspectives hold the truth, think it's our fault. Round and round we go in the circle game of blame and complaint. We'd do better to seek a common ground from which to explore our grievances. We could begin investigating by asking how we can tell what's real and what might be imagined. Such discernment is difficult to accomplish when we believe everything we think and continually perpetuate our storylines. Mindfulness helps us learn to cut through all that divisiveness. Here are the ways:

Recognizing Commonality with Others

You begin to see that all people inhabit a cocoon of habitual patterns that inclines them to certainty that they're right and other people are wrong, or worse, malicious and bad. You see how we all try to find happiness and avoid pain; having seen your own patterns, you can't help seeing how tendencies play out in the lives of others, leading naturally to compassion.

Seeing Beyond Storylines

On issues about which people can seem to inhabit totally different realities, you recognize how such stark differences arise from stories people tell themselves about the world around them. Without losing your ability to discriminate between what's helpful and what is not, you are on the lookout for the good intentions of others, even if you don't agree with their methods.

Inoculating against Hacking

You become aware of the fact that there are people (and organizations, but organizations are made up of people) who are trying to influence the way you think. In the past the media told us what happened and we decided what to think about it. Now, the media tells us what think about something, and we have to decide if actually happened. What you label fake news may depend on your political beliefs but since even real facts are subject to spin, you try to fact check things, not believe everything you read, and allow some space in between your thoughts and actions.

Discovering Society Is Workable

Since society is not something outside of collective individual experiences, you realize that the more you work with your own mind, the better you'll function with others. Seeing the effects of making friends with yourself through meditation, you realize that you'll never change other people's minds by telling them how screwed up they are. Instead you look for common ground and practice patience and exertion, confident that the that the real enemy is confusion and that the world around you is workable.

Inner Reconnaissance:
A Personal Story, Part III

For many years I thought that the best thing I could do to be helpful in this world was to teach Shambhala Training. The curriculum, encompassing more than ten weekend workshops and a two-week residential intensive program, was elegant and all-inclusive. The topic of the first talk of the program was about the basic goodness of existence and of our human nature. The contrarian in me appreciated going against the prevailing cultural perspective which holds that people are the source of pretty much all of the world's woes. Interweaving my own experience with the prescribed logic, I introduced people to Shambhala Training's concept of warriorship.

In this tradition, becoming a warrior means doesn't mean fighting, but rather being beyond war altogether. Practicing gentleness toward ourselves and our world, and fearlessness in being willing to face fear without flinching, warriors learn to exercise intelligence in meeting the challenge of being present in every moment.

More than thirty years of practicing meditation and teaching it to others had made me confident that I knew my own mind. How humbling then, to awaken from a dream one morning while I was on retreat trying to write a book, and for the first time remember a huge childhood trauma. It had been packed away so completely that I had no idea it had ever happened at all.

Humbling indeed. And while the teachings of Shambhala Training unquestionably helped me hold my seat and do the work needed to bring my dark passengers into the light and unpack their baggage, the curriculum didn't tell me how to do it. I had to explore inner space alone, coaxing the light of awareness into long-neglected bodily and energetic nooks and crannies. That is a long story, for another book.

Since this is a short guide to harnessing your own resources to deliver benefit, I'll focus here on what I've found to have the biggest impact, even if the effect is not always immediately apparent. I think of it as taking baby-steps to a better world.

It starts with self-awareness. It takes a certain amount of it to recognize, even after the fact, that one has a tendency to spread one's storms around. To notice an impending squall in time to self-correct, or at least consider the trajectory and potential consequences of what we're about to unleash, we need to be able to direct our attention to our emotional state, detect our inner weather patterns, and discern the most skillful and productive way to respond to our circumstances. Let me offer two small examples.

One day I was feeling productive and full of energy for tackling the day's tasks, which included projects that called for creativity as well as a number of conversations. One of those discussions, early in the day, turned slightly contentious—not a full-fledged argument, but edgy. I briefly interrupted the call to take one from my daughter, whom I very much wanted to talk with. Promising to call her back shortly, I returned to the previous phone meeting. When it ended, I noticed that I felt a little less enthusiasm for the day, as if edginess lingered in the atmosphere, clouding my vision of what to do next.

When I returned my daughter's call, I learned she'd had a minor accident and wasn't really in the mood to talk any more. Hanging up, I felt the cloud of edginess deepening into what seemed like a fog of futility. The day's remaining tasks no longer interested me. I considered reaching back out to one of the people I'd recently talked with in an effort to fix my discomfort, but experience has taught me that in-house repair is more productive.

Had I been in that mood in a formal office environment, I'd probably have gotten busy with something relatively rote, like clearing out my inbox or filing things. But since I work from home and can set my own schedule, and since it was a sunny spring day, I decided to take a short walk. Things were just beginning to bud and bloom in northern Vermont, and as I walked, I watched my attention toggling back and forth between the beauty of the world around me and a nagging sense of unease within me.

That's how it is to be human. We simultaneously inhabit multiple energetic spectrums. In any moment, we may find ourselves anywhere along any of them, from impulsiveness to inertia, from stability to transition, from being inspired to being depressed, from feeling empowered to feeling like a victim. If we recognize and gain familiarity with our energetic patterns, we can learn to see what triggers reactivity and so avoid jumping the gun.

One way of jumping the gun is beating ourselves up over where we happen to be, inner weather-wise. I noticed that tendency on my walk that day: an inner voice kept telling me that I shouldn't let things affect me so much, that I should just get over it and tune back into the gusto I had felt earlier. That is what Trungpa Rinpoche called "negative negativity": not only are we having a hard time, we're making it worse with our strong desire not to be experiencing what we are.

Recognizing that process, I practiced staying present, watching my awareness flitting forth to take in burgeoning fiddlehead ferns, birds busy building nests, blue skies, and my lingering sense of unrest, which seemed to change slightly each time I tuned into it.

It would be nice to be able to say that, as if by magic, when I got back I felt refreshed and ready to dive into the next project. But that wouldn't be true; I started to work and then realized I didn't feel able to muster the creativity necessary for the task at hand. So instead I took care of domestic tasks and mulled over what I might learn from the day's experiences.

After a good night's sleep, I woke ready to tackle the item postponed from the previous day's to-do list: to finish a blog post, of which I'd written only one paragraph. Pondering what direction to go, I felt gratitude for the training in applying mindfulness that had let me ride out my inner weather the day before without allowing my mood to wreak damage in the world around me, and I wrote the story you've just read.

A smaller example is one you may have experienced. It happens where people are lined up, in a hurry, with their own agendas. Airports, hospitals, train stations, pharmacies, almost any government agency: pretty much anywhere in life.

In this case, I was in the checkout line at the grocery store. I don't know if the cashier was brand new or was simply a slow operator, but whatever the case was, she wasn't moving fast enough to suit the woman ahead of me, who seemed to be in a dreadful hurry.

That woman kept sighing as she eyed her groceries creeping along the conveyor belt to be scanned and then passed to a bag boy whose speed was synchronized with that of the cashier. She looked at her watch repeatedly and kept pushing items toward the cashier fast than she was able to scan them. This only succeeded in making the cashier flustered.

Observing this unfolding, I felt sad and began to get a bit anxious myself. Then, without really planning to do anything, I found myself commenting, in a cheerful voice, something along the lines of "Boy, some days are just like that, aren't they?"

In the next instant, several things happened. The cashier shot me a look of gratitude. The impatient woman seemed to realize that she was taking her bad day out on someone else; looking slightly abashed, she said something about being late to pick up her kids. And I relaxed.

We all felt a little better, I think from sharing the understanding that life is sometimes hard, and felt relief in realizing that we don't have to make it worse.

Our days are filled with moments like this, moments offering us opportunities to take baby steps toward a better world. It may not always be safe to intervene; we may know enough to recognize that interceding would only stir things up. Or we might realize too late that an opportunity presented itself and we were too preoccupied to take advantage of it. But the more we notice, the more skillful we get at interrupting the negative momentum within ourselves and in others, and the more we help to cultivate a kinder culture.

See For Yourself

How many times have you told yourself a story that you were certain was true and yet later found it to be false? You confused the order of events, or misheard someone, or simply misremembered. Or maybe after time has passed, you realize you weren't seeing the whole picture. Learning to recognize and question our own stories naturally leads to becoming inquisitive about other people's stories and their influence on behavior.

A powerful factor in how a story plays out is how solidly we believe in the boundaries we've come to accept. While we tend to extend sympathetic attention to those we identify with and project negativity onto "the other," both those categories change constantly. This exercise explores the possibility of expanding our arena of compassionate awareness.

1 First, clear a space by doing a few minutes of mindfulness practice.

2 Now, using the basic contemplation practice as a model, ask yourself, Where are my boundaries?

3 Use these prompts for considering how far you can expand your caring. In each case, if you can, recall or imagine an incident in which someone in that category is at risk of being harmed, either physically or in some less tangible way. Contemplate how protective you feel, and decide how far you would go to prevent harm or to help the following:

- your physical body
- your immediate family
- your extended family
- your closest friends
- friendly acquaintances
- your neighbors
- people in your town
- people in your state
- people in your country
- holders of the same religious beliefs
- those less fortunate than you
- those more fortunate than you

Nationalism's bad reputation in many people's minds arises from its repeated use as an excuse for war. But at least one brilliant historian has argued that from an evolutionary perspective, nationalism is good news. The silver lining reveals itself by considering that homo sapiens evolved in tribes of around a hundred or so members. The boundary was clear; you would fight to support and defend members of your tribe.

With the rise of nationalism, the size of the groups with which humans identify increased into the millions. The radical expansion of boundaries that took people from being willing to fight for a tribe to being willing to fight for a country was enormous. It gives reason to hope that we might actually extend our alliance to the whole of humanity and not have to fight so much at all.

Feel free to explore other categories that make you question your boundaries.

Practice Instructions:
Cultivating a Bigger Perspective

When society is polarized, as it is now, we need to be able to communicate respectfully with others, even if we disagree with their views. This exercise helps tease apart the threads of our reactivity. In the first part, we use bodily sensations, emotions, and our capacity for conceptualization to cultivate our ability to use the body's intelligence to free ourselves from habitual reactions. In the second part, because mindfulness lets us direct and sustain attention, we can use memory and imagination to help us let go of fixed ideas so we can see other people's points of view.

1   First, spend a few minutes in basic mindfulness practice. Set aside for the time being any preoccupations and simply be here. Feel the sense of wakeful presence arising in your stream of being right now.

2   When you've settled, cast your mind back to a time when you apologized to someone after an argument. If you can't remember an actual apology, pick a time when your attitude shifted from certainty that you were right to the recognition that the other person's perspective was at least somewhat valid. (If more than one situation comes to mind, choose the one that holds the most emotional power for you. If you can't remember ever apologizing, contemplate what that tells you about yourself; then try to call to mind a time when you at least softened a previously solid attitude.)

3   When you have a situation in mind, try to remember what it felt like before you decided to apologize, when you were in the middle of the conflict. Recall your certainty, your urge to be right. Can you remember what that felt like? Do you feel that emotion somewhere in your body now? It might be a tightness in your chest, or clenching your hands, or a sensation of heat. Whatever is there, just notice it as fully and completely as you can.

4 Now think back to when you realized you weren't as right as you thought. Did that awareness come to you in a flash, or did it gradually dawn? Was it prompted by an external event, or did your conscience nudge you? Imagine as vividly as you can being back in that moment of deciding to apologize or softening. What do you notice in your body now? Have your inner sensations changed?

Our thoughts, emotions, and bodies are thoroughly intertwined. Science tells us that reactions we think of as being in our minds actually start in our bodies.[1] So paying attention to physical sensations associated with emotions helps us become aware of our habitual ways of reacting. Knowing how it feels in our body to hold fast to solid opinions can serve as a cue to remind us when we might be about to add to the conflict in the world. That awareness allows us to choose our response.

5 Now, to broaden your perspective, contemplate an ongoing interpersonal conflict—one in which you can't understand how the other person can possibly think as they do. There are many possibilities to choose from, aren't there?

It's probably best not to pick the most extreme case. For the purpose of this exercise, choose someone you actually have personal contact with. Take a few moments to consider people you'd like to find new ways of

---

1 Laurie Nummenmaa et al. "Bodily Maps of Emotions." www.ncbi. nlm.nih.gov/pmc/articles/PMC3896150/ January 14, 2014

relating with and choose the one that resonates most right now. We'll call that person the challenger; the challenge they offer is for you to expand your perspective.

6 Imagine yourself sitting face to face with the challenger. As you picture this, pay attention to your body, especially any areas where you noticed feeling something during the conflict part of the earlier contemplation. Is there a similar feeling or something different?

7 Next, if you can, picture switching places with the challenger. Try to imagine that you hold their perspective on the situation and are facing someone who holds your view. Remember the feeling of being right in the last exercise, wherever you noticed it in your body, and see if you can feel it again, but this time from the challenger's point of view, being triggered by you and your views. Don't worry if this feels hard or even impossible. Even trying to put yourself in the challenger's place will stretch your awareness and may bring insight.

Whether you were successful in imagining switching places or not, stop now and notice what you feel in your body. Now think back again to the last exercise: can you recall the sensations you felt in your body when you remembered apologizing or softening your position?

That's the feeling of letting go.

8 Finally, imagine sitting with your challenger again, but this time imagine the scene from above. With a bird's eye view of the two of you sitting face to face, let your body relax into the feeling of letting go.

Do you see the situation in a new light? Without struggling to find an answer, be open to any fresh insights that may arise about that situation.

9 Now take a moment and see if you can think of a gesture of openness that you would be willing to make to move that situation forward. Ask yourself if there's anything further for you to learn from this exercise. The ability to expand your perspective, especially in highly charged situations, naturally progresses in fits and starts, so don't be discouraged. When situations are particularly sticky, you might find it helpful to repeat this exercise periodically or even regularly.

10 As always, end your exercise by spending a few minutes resting in wakeful presence.

Society's Stories

Society starts with one-on-one interactions. If you're ignorant of the storylines you've inherited and maintain, your interactions with others are more likely to add to confusion than to help bring about a better world. Paying attention to your mental contents and storylines creates space that gives you the freedom to shift toward more collaborative perspectives and interactions.

The stories we tell ourselves about human society evolve over generations. Now that we realize the damage rigid and biased views—about race, appropriate roles for genders, and sexual preferences, to name but a few—can cause, we've become more tolerant. But the social tectonic shift that moved a culture from separate drinking fountains for different races to gender neutral bathrooms in one lifetime has not only destroyed old forms, its aftershocks are shaking the inner lives of some members of that society, solidifying the stories we tell about one another.

Mindfulness undermines the solidity of those stories. Seeing how our own patterns operate brings clarity that allows us to see how they operate within others and in the world at large, letting us more objectively analyze and evaluate situations and rousing, instead of old complaints, fresh inspiration: How can I help?

We start by recognizing that the petty, snarky, greedy, ruthless, unkind, narcissistic, belligerent, and otherwise generally nasty stuff that so often gets called "human nature" arises out of an energetic field we all inhabit. We're largely unaware of its influence on our lives until we start paying attention to how our patterns shift: from impulsiveness to inertia, from stability to transition, from being inspired to being depressed, from feeling empowered to feeling like a victim. Gaining familiarity with these energetic patterns, we can learn to see what triggers reactivity and so can avoid adding to the conflicts in society.

We help even more by learning to rest in wakeful presence—which is our basic nature and also the basic nature of the universe—and thus allowing our lives to reflect the inherent underlying harmony that accommodates all apparent phenomena and the whole of existence. As more people begin to harness their inner resources in this way, society will naturally begin to reflect that harmony as well.

Observing your mind with discipline, you become more adept at detecting its changing patterns and a sneaking suspicion begins to dawn: the identity you've believed in for so long may not be not as solid as you thought.

Dealing With Duality

And so you come back to the perennial question, Who am I?

For now, let's postulate this: your basic nature is wakeful presence imbued with sense perceptions. Identifying that as a "self," we begin splitting experience apart. We call the one registering perceptions "I" and the content of those perceptions "other." This process is so ingrained and habitual that most of us, if we think of it at all, consider it an inherent and inevitable part of being human. Duality seems to be the way of the world.

But it is this fixation on duality—with "I" as the subject experiencing everything else as the object—that makes our mostly empty world seem so solid. This fixation turns a field of constantly changing energetic flux into what appears to be empty space chock full of lots of separate stuff and inhabited by our own dear discrete selves.

The rapid ping-ponging back and forth of perception between the ongoing awareness we experience as "me" and the panoramic display we call "the world" creates the illusion of solidity. We maintain the illusion with self-narratives about our personal history, continually referring to the memory of our perception of that solidity in the past and hopeful or fearful anticipation about how we may encounter it in the future.

It works a little like a movie. The light of awareness shines through rapidly changing patterns projecting in space—that would be us—to create apparent phenomena. I heard a story once about a group of Tibetans who were watching a movie for the first time. They got agitated as it became clear that a character in the film was about to do some dastardly deed. Finally, one man could stand it no longer. He stood up and charged the screen, yelling, "Stop now!"

Thanks to the power of momentum in personal and cultural habitual patterns, many humans find ourselves feeling trapped, playing roles in movies we don't remember choosing. We won't free ourselves from that condition by battling the world, or even by trying to change ourselves. It's like attacking the screen to alter the movie. It's too late at that point: it's already in the can.

We need get involved at an earlier level, to come up with a winning concept and help develop a decent script. Thinking of ourselves as vehicles for delivering benefit can turn life into a win-win game of improvisation.

Seeing our patterns is the first step to freeing ourselves from the momentum of confusion maintained by energetic patterns embedded in our bodies.

Engaging Energy

To deliver benefit into the world, we need to tune into our bodies' patterns of energy. Start by considering the experience of being embodied. (If you like, stop reading right now and close your eyes for a moment. Feel what it feels like, being in your body.) You might be aware of being hot or cold, hungry or hurting. Or you could be like so many of us, and not feel very much at all. At least not much to speak about.

That's because, unless we're in pain, what we notice when we turn our attention inward is energy, which is hard to talk about. We may not even understand what we're looking for. In the beginning, if we're lucky enough to become aware of anything at all, we might notice energy as a feeling, like being tired, or antsy, or invigorated, or numb, or something we can't quite put our finger on.

That's how it is with energy: when we try to pin it down, we discover its inexpressible aspect. It can't be easily described, but with training we can learn to discern the experience of it. And then, discriminating the interactions occurring between our bodies, our emotions, and our thought process, we can learn to ride life's energies instead of being buffeted around by them.

To deconstruct this thing called a self, let's look at how our experience of it comes together. In our experience, the three systems pointed to with the triangle diagram on page 72, our bodily sensations, emotions, and thoughts, are inseparable from each other and from wakeful presence. But when inattention and the momentum of conditioning prevent our experiencing the space of wakeful presence, the different functions of body and mind go unrecognized and undisciplined. And so our potentially valuable resources instead collude with great lifelong consistency to create a perfect storm of confusion.

Let's consider how this happens. Your body provides a physical platform for consciousness and monitors the inner state of that platform to maintain homeostasis. It also retains archival storage of unprocessed life events; those will linger until they're brought to the light of awareness and accepted for what they are, or until the carrier buys the farm and all property is returned to universal inventory, whichever comes first.

Your body's star turn on stage is as ambassador to the world: sense perceptions team up with the brain to deliver information about your environment and cohorts. When it's time to do something about what you know, your body accomplishes it. In both those ways, as a window on the world and as an agent of activity, your body supports your sense of self.

Your subconscious also functions as a window, but the realm it opens onto is an energetic one. It's what we've been calling inner space, the unseen infrastructure of the material world, and the inhabitants therein. It's a place known to most of us only through symbols washed up on the shores of dreams, or emotions overpowering or steering our courses with their ceaseless undercurrents. We call people with relatively reliable connections here psychic; all of us have, from time to time, intuitive hunches. But without training to lift our habitual blinds so we can access such information, this is one glass through which we truly do see darkly.

Now imagine that wakeful presence, which permeates all experience, has gotten trapped by discursive mind in between those two windows. Conscious mind is the thinker we're usually aware of, the part that discriminates one thing from another, that organizes things conceptually and keeps track of our storyline: who we are; our goals, relationships, history, and preferences; how we're doing. This is the part that talks pretty much non-stop, as we quickly notice when we start trying to sit still and be present for five minutes.

In the untrained person, attention is scattered. Once you learn how to direct its power to gather and focus the light of awareness, you can choose how to use this capacity: you might exude beneficent warmth, like the sun, or cut to the heart of the matter with laser-like precision. Untrained people, like pinball machines flashing "TILT", are all over the place.

So the light of awareness is like the bulb in a projector, only instead of displaying a film that's already complete, it's shining through the content of each moment. And moments go by so fast, and there's so much to process, that it seems seamless, just like a movie does on the screen.

But here's the thing. Remember those two windows: the window on the world that the senses offer and the window on inner space the subconscious and intuition open? Now think about what happens at night when you turn the light on in a room with bare glass windows. Instead of being transparent, windows then become like mirrors. Not only can you not see out very easily, but images in the room are reflected back to you, as if in a mirror—a solipsistic paradise.

As long as our attention is enslaved by discursive mind sitting in between these two lenses, the light of awareness stays focused on mind's busy activities. Then, instead of offering accurate vistas of the outer world and inner space, our windows become a kaleidoscope of reflections and projections, and our stream of consciousness, bouncing around riding herd on it all, confirms by all the busyness its assumption that a self truly exists.

Smoke, Mirrors, and Momentum

The only true continuity to be found is wakeful presence. If it is held captive in a case of mistaken identification, buffeted about by tendencies, and buffered from the genuine experience of life by a cocoon of habitual patterns, when we look out at the world, we don't see clearly what's actually there. Instead of seeing things as they are, we see things as they appear through the filters of our storylines, our opinions, our beliefs, our passengers' biases and their unexplored baggage.

Obstructions to seeing clearly include everything from adopted social norms (original sin is our human inheritance; it's a dog-eat-dog world, so eat first; there's only One Truth and we have it) to internalized emotional assumptions based on experiences (I'm stupid and unworthy; there's never enough to go around; no matter what I do, somebody will bail me out; they'd better, because I'm the victim here!), to trauma imbedded in our tissues that rouses anxiety's alarm needlessly. There's no limit to the amount of baggage we can bring on board.

But we pay a price for it. Confusion does indeed have its cost and in this case it's stress, anxiety, and exhaustion. As we struggle to juggle our baggage, life goes on within us and without us. The only way *I* can keep up is by completely disregarding the complexity of internal and external reality, instead carving things up into bite-size chunks.

With the best of intentions, *I* courts confusion, sustaining itself by the processes of reification, identification, and projection. Reification occurs when we solidify a person, place, or process into a thing. Identification takes place when we get possessive about some of those things and feel like they're part of us. Armed with those two, and enlisting the help of their pal, projection, *I* tackles the world, spewing smoke and opinions left and right.

Projection is the great switcheroo wherein we take something—often it's something we don't want to face, but it can be something we're strongly attached to —in ourselves and pin it on somebody else. Everybody is familiar with projection and most people think it's something only other people do—a splendid example of projection.

Through projection we divide the world into us and them and go to town. With emotional demons, balloons of bias, discursive dust-devils, and the grinding of attitudinal axes all rattling around in the funhouse of our lives, it's no wonder we're convinced there's someone home.

This, then, is how the self we take for granted works: smoke, mirrors, and momentum. Habitual conceptual activity bounces off paired but distorted reflections: bodily sensations delivering information about the world and subconscious impressions of the energies of inner space. This process creates a hall of mirrors wherein more tales than Scheherazade ever dreamed of are woven together, a cloud of cocoons.

Then, because we don't take time to stop and examine our experience, those tales are told and retold and passed down like family heirlooms. Baggage to hold onto.

Of course I exist. I'm talking aren't I?

Delivering The Goods

Of course, I do exist, talking or not. But to cut through the troublesome triad of reification, identification, and projection, it helps to think of ourselves as not so solidly separate. This is where the metaphor of humans as vehicles is helpful. We all know life is a trip and it's reasonable to ask, How's your vehicle? What do you convey into this world through your thoughts, words, and deeds?

We live in challenging times for which we have responsibility. Human beings convey within us attitudes, inclinations, and the unfinished business of previous generations. Our lack of awareness about what we carry perpetuates age-old conflicts.

But properly trained and put to good use, the nature of our awareness gives us the power to meet not only the challenges we face presently, but to alleviate the suffering of future generations. Not knowing this, we fail to fulfill our beneficial potential. In our ignorance, we may bring even more misery to ourselves and others.

Some of the pain human beings experience can't be escaped; it's inherent in existence by virtue of the uncertainty and impermanence that are built into the physical system. We will all experience bodily discomfort. We will all suffer losses and grieve. We will all die. These are not facts to avoid, but realities to navigate. If we learn how, instead of life being a minefield we tiptoe through, it becomes a dancing ground of celebration. We appreciate it even more for its poignancy. When inevitable pain comes to us, it reminds us that we're alive and able to open to experience fully.

But much of the pain we suffer isn't the unavoidable kind. Rather we create it for ourselves by not knowing that we're vehicles as opposed to solid discrete individuals. Instead of connecting with our basic nature so that we can deliver harmony and health into the world, we get carried away by confusion. And to compound matters, we fail to recognize it as such and are sure we're right. This inevitably puts us at odds with other people who don't agree with us and are sure they're right.

But an evolutionary vanguard is emerging: people who learn to apply mindfulness, a skill inherent in us all but largely latent until we meet our minds and cut through confusion. We do this by learning to direct and sustain our attention, detect the patterns that exist within us and around us, and discern the behavior that will bring the greatest benefit in any given moment.

We're inspired to help because when we're unencumbered by habitual patterns that we thought comprised the "self" we've worked so hard to maintain, we feel less solid. We begin to intuit how we're connected to every other person inhabiting planet Earth, We realize that rather than being a zero-sum game, life is an energetic collaboration and every one of us has a contribution to make to the ongoing experiment in conscious evolution that is humanity.

Understanding this, we are on our way to unlocking the wealth of the greatest natural resource on earth, which we will only find by exploring our inner experience. Are you up for the challenge?

Further Tools to Help You Deliver Benefit

Below are some big topics, the exploration of any of which could easily fill a separate book; these practice steps hint at how, as you become adept at applying mindfulness, you can use the basic contemplative technique to help bring your best into any situation. Feel free to adapt these instructions as your intuition suggests.

Treating the Trickster

Fear is a trickster because it wears many masks: anger, despair, jealousy, greed. Busyness is often a way of avoiding fear. Depression can serve to numb the experience of fear. Exploring your cocoon will give you the most information about what your particular passengers fear; it could be loss, failure, success, etc. Deepest of all, for most of us, lies a fear of death. Whenever you find yourself getting solid, let that be a cue to ask yourself if there's something you're afraid of in that moment.

If you can take the time to touch in and connect with something, use these steps to work with it:

1 Find the fear feeling in your body; this is easier to do on the fly if you've spent some time in quiet contemplation of fear.

2 Stay present with whatever sensations you have; notice any storyline that arises and see if you can let it go and come back to simple experience.

3 Go forward with fear as your companion; often the only difference between fear and excitement is your attitude .and if you change your attitude and relax as it is, you can use fear's energy to fuel your engagement.

Mindful Communication:

The Key to Creating Community

Learning to listen mindfully and interrupt reactivity's momentum is essential if society is to cohere, comprised as it is of people with radically different ideas about so many things. Mr. Rogers said his mother told him, when confronted with scary news, to look for the helpers.

Here are a few steps to help you be one of those:

1 STOW YOUR STORYLINE—stop and drop into wakeful presence.

2 OPEN EARS AND MIND—see patterns arise and let them go.

3 REALLY LISTEN—within and without, setting aside reactions or judgments.

4 SPEAK CLEARLY AND KINDLY—tell the truth gently, with awarewness of what we have in common.

Meditation in Action:
Stop, Drop, and Roll

As you become more confident in recognizing the contrast between being present and being caught up in thought, you will begin to notice it more and more throughout your life, even when you aren't practicing formal meditation. Use that recognition of contrast as a reminder that even if you can't create temporal or physical space, you can still .

STOP—interrupt your own momentum by taking a conscious breath.

DROP—allow your awareness to drop into your body and feel what it feels like to be here, now.

ROLL—step freshly into the next moment as unencumbered as possible.

Don't be hard on yourself. Even picking up this book is a big step. At this point in time, out of all the people in the world, you are one of the few who realize the value of looking inward and working with your mind. Realizing that not every thought that occurs in your mind is true is a radical insight.

People who continue to entrench themselves in habitual patterns, convinced that the problem lies somewhere outside of themselves, won't be very helpful in dealing with the challenges facing humanity, now and in the future. Even trying to meditate is doing something to move the species forward along a positive trajectory. Meeting your mind and making friends with yourself is the surest way to a meaningful life.

So keep going. Don't stop with the methods in this book. Because wisdom arises from space and space is everywhere, there's no limit to what you can explore. If you nurture your inherent curiosity, you will no doubt discover tools that will enable you to harness the world's greatest resource, the power of good that is the natural essence of the human heart.

GLOSSARY

Glossary

ATTENTION — our ability to focus; noticing where our awareness is directed

AWARENESS — our inherent capacity for perception of outer and inner phenomena

BAGGAGE — emotional and energetic damage carried within our bodies and psyches long after whatever conflict or trauma precipitated the reaction

BODILY SENSATIONS — data about the external world delivered by our senses as well as proprioceptive and energetic information that comes from directing attention to inner space

COCOON – the filter of habitual patterns maintained by recreating familiar patterns of behavior and thought to solidify our sense of self and ward off fear of uncertainty and the groundlessness of space; our passengers inhabit the cocoon and shore up with baggage a sense of separateness

CONDITIONING — learned or inherited patterns of behavior; can give rise to the experience of being on autopilot and not fully inhabiting one's life

CONTEMPLATION — a technique of directing attention to inner space in order to invite insight to arise

HABITUAL PATTERNS — conditioned ways we tend to behave or respond, ranging from minor tics to major personality components; whereas habits can be consciously cultivated in order to free up attention when engaging in mundane tasks, habitual patterns are generally unconscious and interfere with the clear perception of situations

INNER RECONNAISSANCE — exploring inner space though gentle but persistent inquisitiveness to detect patterns of thoughts, emotions, and bodily sensations that shape the way we experience reality; the process of becoming aware of our passengers and baggage

Inner Space — the realm inhabited by consciousness, accessible to us by learning to rest in wakeful presence and direct out attention impartially to whatever arises

Intellect — the faculty enabling us to reason; the ability to analyze conceptually

Intuition — the spontaneous arising of wisdom or understanding without conscious reasoning

Meditation — the continual act of making friends with yourself; the discipline of learning to notice the difference between being caught up in thoughts and simply resting in wakeful presence, cultivated by practicing mindfulness

Mindfulness — the ability to direct and sustain our attention on whatever we choose, cultivated by repeatedly bringing the focus of awareness to a chosen object

Passengers — persistent and recurrent inner tendencies; habitual motivations, defenses, and distractions within us that express themselves through repeated thoughts

Reactivity — unthinking conditioned reflexive response to a challenge, conflict, or provocation

Stories – agreements we make in order to communicate; explanations we give to justify our actions and reactions

Storylines — the weaving together of stories to interpret the world and ascribe meaning; the things we tell ourselves about who we are which become a filter through which we see the world

Wakeful Presence — the underlying ground of human existence; experienced as a state of simple awareness in the moment

EXERCISES

Basic Mindfulness Practice

A Few Tips before You Begin:

Find a quiet, comfortable place to sit. This could be on a cushion on the floor or in a chair with your feet flat on the ground.

It's a good idea to set a timer. Ten minutes is good to start, although if you can't manage that, even five will begin to help you meet your mind and strengthen your mindfulness muscle.

In this type of meditation, it's good to keep your eyes open, with a slightly downward, soft or unfocused gaze. The reason for this is that we live our lives with our eyes open and meditation is not a retreat from life; keeping your eyes open facilitates mindful transitions between sitting practice and the rest of your day.

1 Sit. Settle into a comfortable position. If you're on a cushion, your legs can be crossed on the floor in front of you. Knees should be below your hips. Sit up straight without being rigid, with a strong back and a soft front. Let your hands settle naturally on your thighs. Don't be afraid to adjust your position as you go. Meditation is not an endurance test.

2 Settle. Bring your attention to what it feels like to be sitting in this particular space in this particular body in this particular moment. Allow yourself to feel your weight of your body on the cushion or chair. What do you notice? What physical sensations do you

feel? Perhaps there is tension somewhere in your body. You might notice sense perceptions — a nearby sound or the temperature in the room. Whatever you notice, just allow your attention to be on the simple experience of being present in your body right now.

3 ATTENTION ON BREATH. Once you've settled, it's time to bring your attention to a reference point in the present. There are many possible choices but the simplest is your breath, because it's always with you and it's hard to work up too many thoughts about it. See where you notice your breath most clearly in your body. For some people it's in the rising and falling of the chest and abdomen; for others it's in the sensation of the breath as it passes through the nostrils. Wherever it is for you, spend some time simply noticing the breath as you inhale and exhale.

4 DISTRACTION. This isn't actually an instruction, but more an acknowledgement of what's bound to happen. Thoughts will arise and at some point you'll notice that you've forgotten all about your breath. That's fine! That's actually the whole point—learning to notice when we are thinking, and then practicing coming back to our chosen focus.

5 COME BACK! Actually, at the moment you notice that you've been thinking, you're already back in the present. So just redirect your attention to the breath. Continue cycling through steps 3 – 5, coming back to the breath with gentle persistence, until the timer goes off.

Try to Sit at Least 10 Minutes a Day

You can sit for longer if you like, but it's important not to set unrealistic goals, since failing to meet those goals is extremely disheartening. It's important to sit for the whole amount of time you've set for yourself, and it's helpful to sit at the same time every day, so that it becomes a part of your routine.

Keep A Record Of Your Practice In A Journal

As soon as your ten minutes are up, write in your journal the date and note how long your sat down and meditated. Then just write a few words that come to mind to describe the experience. It could be as simple as "sleepy" or "agitated." Or you might note "Couldn't stop thinking about work." This is a great tool for beginning to track your patterns and hold yourself accountable.

If you remember something important that you need to do after you get up, you can make a quick note about it so you don't get stuck trying to hold on to those thoughts. You can jot them down and get back to your practice.

If you miss a day or two, don't beat yourself up. Just come back!

Basic Inner Space Exploration

Deliberate investigation can help us understand the nature of the inner processes that shapes our lives. Only through open inquisitiveness will we, like Lewis and Clark, gain access to the intelligence native to that territory.

1 Begin with basic mindfulness practice until you feel somewhat settled. Then close your eyes and bring your awareness into your body.

2 What do you notice? Physical sensations like your weight on the chair or cushion, or the temperature of the air? Sounds or other phenomena delivered through your sense perceptions without any effort on your part? Tightness or pain in any part of your body?

3 Try dropping a little more deeply into your body, letting the light of awareness move like a spotlight throughout your interior. Remembering that your body is energy that has temporarily coalesced in space, pay attention to how energy feels within you—where it flows and where it's stuck. Perhaps several different parts of your body feel connected in some way, even if you can't tell how. Just notice what's there to be noticed, and if you can't feel some parts of your body from the inside, that's useful intelligence too.

4 See if a particular area in your body wants your attention during this period of time; if nothing particular catches your attention, pick an area that you can feel.

5 Now ask an inner question: what wisdom or pain is this sensation holding? Don't grasp for an answer but just allow space for insight to arise. If the idea of passengers resonates with you, try this question: who is on board that wants the spotlight today? Again, wait. Patience is key.

Once you get the hang of exploring inner space, there are techniques that can help you clear the baggage that passengers carry. This liberates energy that's trapped in compensatory and habitual tendencies. But the first thing you need to do is to get a sense of the constellation of energetic inclinations and propensities that form your inner firmament.

Basic Contemplation Practice

The purpose of contemplation practice is to harness the power of the conceptual mind. We all have wisdom within that we normally don't have access to because our minds stay so busy—thinking about work, or a conversation we had last week, or what we had for breakfast; there's no space for wisdom to arise.

This Practice Is Useful in Many Situations:

- when something's bothering us and we don't know what it is
- when we have a situation that we're not sure what to do about
- when we want to clarify our goals
- when we would like to bring more clarity and insight into the process of making a decision or understanding an experience

Ideally you would find a quiet place to do this practice and have at least ten or fifteen uninterrupted minutes; that's creating physical and temporal space. As for creating mental space to allow insight to arise.

These Are the Steps:

Clear a space with basic mindfulness practice.

1   Clear a space with basic mindfulness practice.

2   Bring to mind a question or an issue. Ask yourself what would be helpful to know.

3   Be patient and inquisitive without an agenda.

4   Set aside the first answer that comes up.

5   Go back and see if you can go a little deeper. Ask yourself if there's anything further that it would be helpful to know.

One of the biggest obstacles to insight arising is our impatience to have an answer. Don't struggle for it, let it come to you. If you create space, insight can arise.

Practice Instructions:
Cultivating a Bigger Perspective

When society is polarized, as it is now, we need to be able to communicate respectfully with others, even if we disagree with their views. This exercise helps tease apart the threads of our reactivity. In the first part, we use bodily sensations, emotions, and our capacity for conceptualization to cultivate our ability to use the body's intelligence to free ourselves from habitual re-actions. In the second part, because mindfulness lets us direct and sustain attention, we can use memory and imagination to help us let go of fixed ideas so we can see other people's points of view.

1   First, spend a few minutes in basic mindfulness prac-tice. Set aside for the time being any preoccupations and simply be here. Feel the sense of wakeful presence arising in your stream of being right now.

2   When you've settled, cast your mind back to a time when you apologized to someone after an argu-ment. If you can't remember an actual apology, pick a time when your attitude shifted from certainty that you were right to the recognition that the other person's per-spective was at least somewhat valid. (If more than one situation comes to mind, choose the one that holds the most emotional power for you. If you can't remember ever apologizing, contemplate what that tells you about yourself; then try to call to mind a time when you at least softened a previously solid attitude.)

3   When you have a situation in mind, try to re-
    member what it felt like before you decided to
apologize, when you were in the middle of the conflict. Recall your certainty, your urge to be right. Can
you remember what that felt like? Do you feel that
emotion somewhere in your body now? It might be a
tightness in your chest, or clenching your hands, or a
sensation of heat. Whatever is there, just notice it as
fully and completely as you can.

4   Now think back to when you realized you weren't
    as right as you thought. Did that awareness come
to you in a flash, or did it gradually dawn? Was it
prompted by an external event, or did your conscience
nudge you? Imagine as vividly as you can being back
in that moment of deciding to apologize or softening.
What do you notice in your body now? Have your inner
sensations changed?

Our thoughts, emotions, and bodies are thoroughly intertwined. Science tells us that reactions we
think of as being in our minds actually start in our
bodies. So paying attention to physical sensations associated with emotions helps us become aware of our
habitual ways of reacting. Knowing how it feels in
our body to hold fast to solid opinions can serve as a
cue to remind us when we might be about to add to
the conflict in the world. That awareness allows us to
choose our response.

5 Now, to broaden your perspective, contemplate an ongoing interpersonal conflict—one in which you can't understand how the other person can possibly think as they do. There are many possibilities to choose from, aren't there?

It's probably best not to pick the most extreme case. For the purpose of this exercise, choose someone you actually have personal contact with. Take a few moments to consider people you'd like to find new ways of relating with and choose the one that resonates most right now. We'll call that person the challenger; the challenge they offer is for you to expand your perspective.

6 Imagine yourself sitting face to face with the challenger. As you picture this, pay attention to your body, especially any areas where you noticed feeling something during the conflict part of the earlier contemplation. Is there a similar feeling or something different?

7 Next, if you can, picture switching places with the challenger. Try to imagine that you hold their perspective on the situation and are facing someone who holds your view. Remember the feeling of being right in the last exercise, wherever you noticed it in your body, and see if you can feel it again, but this time from the challenger's point of view, being triggered by you and your views. Don't worry if this feels hard or even impossible. Even trying to put yourself in the challenger's place will stretch your awareness and may bring insight.

Whether you were successful in imagining switching places or not, stop now and notice what you feel in your body. Now think back again to the last exercise: can you recall the sensations you felt in your body when you remembered apologizing or softening your position? That's the feeling of letting go.

8 Finally, imagine sitting with your challenger again, but this time imagine the scene from above. With a bird's eye view of the two of you sitting face to face, let your body relax into the feeling of letting go.

Do you see the situation in a new light? Without struggling to find an answer, be open to any fresh insights that may arise about that situation.

9 Now take a moment and see if you can think of a gesture of openness that you would be willing to make to move that situation forward.

Ask yourself if there's anything further for you to learn from this exercise.

The ability to expand your perspective, especially in highly charged situations, naturally progresses in fits and starts, so don't be discouraged. When situations are particularly sticky, you might find it helpful to repeat this exercise periodically or even regularly.

10 As always, end your exercise by spending a few minutes resting in wakeful presence.

Working with Fear

1 Find the fear feeling in your body; this is easier to do on the fly if you've spent some time in quiet contemplation of fear.

2 Stay present with whatever sensations you have; notice any storyline that arises and see if you can let it go and come back to simple experience.

3 Go forward with fear as your companion; often the only difference between fear and excitement is your attitude and if you change your attitude and relax as it is, you can use fear's energy to fuel your engagement.

Communicating Mindfully:

1 STOW YOUR STORYLINE—stop and drop into wakeful presence.

2 OPEN EARS AND MIND—see patterns arise and let them go.

3 REALLY LISTEN—within and without, setting aside reactions/judgments.

4 SPEAK CLEARLY AND KINDLY—telling the truth gently, appreciating commonality

Applying Mindfulness on the Go: Stop, Drop, and Roll

Stop—interrupt your own momentum by taking a conscious breath.

Drop—allow your awareness to drop into your body and feel what it feels like to be here, now.

Roll—step freshly into the next moment as unencumbered as possible.

Attending to the Body

Our bodies carry us through time and space and enable us to act in the world. They deserve our attention for those reasons, but also because the body is a storehouse of unprocessed reactivity. Everything from trauma to simple discomfort prompts unconscious energetic and muscular holding patterns that we tend not to notice at all. To the extent they do arise in our awareness, we may think something like, "I hold a lot of tension in my neck," or "Sometimes my back just goes out for no apparent reason."

A simple body scan will help you recognize the places in your body where you have blockages; you can find a simple body scan and other guided meditation instructions at www.uclahealth.org/marc/mindful-meditations

A further tool in inner reconnaissance is to attend to the felt sense we have of being in our bodies; a technique called Focusing can be helpful in bringing to light underlying causes of patterns and the wisdom trapped therein. Instructions can be found at www.focusing.org/index.htm

More physically active tools are beneficial as well. Yoga, Tai Chi, Qi Gong are contemplative movement practices that help synchronize body and mind and release energetic blockages that have accrued throughout time. Groups working with these techniques can be found in most communities.

And although I mention it last it is certainly not least: never underestimate the physical and psychological benefits of taking a walk outside!

Find Audio and Video Versions of Many of These Exercises on Applied Mindfulness Training's Website:

www.appliedmindfulnesstraining.org/
mindfulness-and-meditation-exercises

Exercises from
The Inner Advantage
by Patton Hyman

Exercise 1: Listening to Yourself

In this exercise recite something that you know by heart. It can be the "Pledge of Allegiance," the Lord's Prayer," a favorite poem, your family's traditional grace before meals, or a passage from your own particular religious background. Just make sure that it's something familiar because the point of this exercise is to bring your attention to your own speaking and not to have to struggle with memory of the particular passage. Here's the exercise:

Do this privately. Start with a few minutes of mindfulness meditation to come back into connection with presence, and then recite the passage in your normal speaking voice and at an ordinary pace—no need to get dramatic, just speak ordinarily. Listen to the sound of your voice, and if you find yourself thinking, whether it's about how you sound or what you're going to have for lunch, simply come back to listening to yourself. Pause for a few moments, resting in the experience of presence. Repeat the exercise as many times as you like. Then just let it go. If you do this, for example, near the end of a meditation session, leave yourself a few minutes at the end to meditate simply.

Takeaway: This exercise will help you recognize that distraction is a very ordinary experience and that it's possible to stay present while you're speaking.

Exercise 2: The Telephone Practice

This is a practice to do at work and is especially useful if you use the phone frequently. It's simply this: when the phone rings (or when you're about to pick up the phone to make a call), put your hand on it and pause for a moment (one ring's worth will do) and notice the experience of presence. Then pick up the phone and proceed. If you use a cell phone, you may want to place it face down so that you don't immediately see who is calling and start thinking about what you'll say.

Takeaway: This exercise will help you recognize that presence is available in completely routine situations, without the need for extensive preparation.

Exercise 3: Focusing and Opening

Find a clean and clear space where you can do this exercise and bring along an object to use in the exercise. It can be a flower, a fruit, a stone, a dish, or whatever you have handy. After doing a few minutes of mindfulness meditation to connect with presence, pay attention to the object for a few moments. Then broaden your gaze so that you connect with whatever is in your field of vision. During any part of this, if you find yourself distracted by thoughts, simply come back to focusing on your chosen object, and after a few moments, again open your gaze into your field of vision.

Pause for a few moments, resting in the experience of presence. Repeat the exercise several times if you have time.

TAKEAWAY: This exercise will familiarize you with the difference between focusing your gaze and opening it as if it's the aperture of a wide-angle camera. Unlike Exercise 1, this exercise is silent, so as you become more familiar with it, you can do it in any situation. It's probably easiest with the visual sense, which is so vivid; however, you can also do it with hearing or other sensory perceptions.

Exercise 4: 360° Awareness

After doing a few minutes of mindfulness meditation to connect with presence, stand in place with an open focus of your gaze, relaxing into your field of vision. Slowly rotate in place allowing whatever comes into your field of vision to be registered in your awareness, like a camera scanning the horizon. If you find yourself focusing on any particular item that comes into view, just relax into your broad field of vision. During any part of this, if you find yourself distracted by thoughts, simply come back to the exercise. When you reach your starting point, stand there with your vision open.

TAKEAWAY: Like Exercise 2, this exercise will familiarize you with the experience of unfixated vision and the ability to distinguish it from staring at a particular spot or object, which is another form of distraction (if it's not done intentionally). The difference is that you'll be doing this while you're in motion. You will notice that this is available in any situation, not just one of formal practice.

Exercise 5: Taking a Walk

After doing a few minutes of mindfulness meditation, find a pleasant place to take a walk for 10 or 15 minutes, or longer if you like. Decide in advance how long you'll walk, and then just walk, avoiding any particular agenda, whether it's finding mushrooms, identifying plants and trees, recognizing geological formations, or whatever. Just walk with your vision, hearing, and other senses open, taking in whatever you encounter. If you find yourself distracted by thoughts, simply let go of them and come back to walking with open awareness. If you encounter other people, relate to them as you ordinarily would (the idea is not to seem like a weirdo), and when they're gone, come back to this walking exercise. When your walking time is over, return to your starting point where you did the initial mindfulness meditation. Notice whether anything changes about your state of mind and awareness of presence after you consider the exercise to be completed.

TAKEAWAY: This exercise is intended to broaden your scope of applying mindfulness so that presence is available in a variety of situations.

Exercise 6: Speaking to (and Listening to) another Person

This exercise is done with a partner, someone who is willing to do a mindfulness exercise with you. A person who is already involved with mindfulness discipline will be helpful. As with Exercise 1, find a quiet and private place for the exercise and begin with a few minutes of meditation to firm up the connection with presence. Decide who will go first and decide on a time; if possible, set a timer so nobody has to keep glancing at a watch. The first to speak has two tasks: the first is to listen to his or her own voice (see Exercise1); the second is to be aware of any emotional tone (including fear or nervousness) experienced while speaking, including during any gaps in the speaking. The listener (who only listens and doesn't talk) has three tasks: one is to listen to the other person's voice; another is to be aware of any distractedness from listening; and the third is to be aware of any emotional tone (including fear or nervousness) experienced while listening to the other person.

TAKEAWAY: This exercise ups the mindfulness ante by working to cultivate mindfulness while relating to another person. Issues of distractedness and emotional tone are clarified by this exercise.

Exercise 7: Listening to Music

This exercise can be done alone or with other people. As usual, start with a few minutes of meditation to clarify the connection with presence. In this exercise, listen to a variety of kinds of music and notice the emotional tone evoked by each and how they're different. My preference is for instrumental music since there is less likelihood of getting caught up in the words, but you may have a different preference. The important factor here is to use a variety of different kinds of music, and a digital device may allow you to pre-select a number of album cuts so that you don't have to interrupt the listening experience by changing CDs or vinyl records; if that's not available, just remember to continue in presence as you make those changes.

Takeaway: This exercise focuses on recognizing emotional responses to nonverbal stimuli, recognizing how your response to a particular artist or composer or type of music differs from your response to others. Don't over-analyze; just enjoy the experience; you may notice things you hadn't noticed before. You may also notice changes in your musical taste, finding that you actually enjoy opera or hip-hop when previously you thought that you couldn't abide it!

Exercise 8: Driving Your Car
(or Riding Public Transportation)

Because you can connect with presence in any situation, finding a regular time for that (aside from formal sitting practice) can be helpful. Because most of us travel to work daily, using that time can be helpful in establishing the universal availability of presence. If you're driving to work, just turn off the radio or stereo and notice how you can be present in the car as it moves down the road. With presence, you'll notice the landscape around you (whether constructed or natural), details about your vehicle, and whatever else comes to your attention. Make it a relaxed experience without trying to hold tightly to any of those experiences; just let them happen naturally. If you're taking public transportation (whether bus, train, or airplane), turn off your electronic equipment and notice your surroundings, both within the vehicle—other passengers—and outside.

TAKEAWAY: This exercise will help you see that you can connect with presence anywhere, anytime.

ACKNOWLEDGEMENTS

This book grew out of a series of classes presented at the St. Johnsbury Athenaeum in the Northeast Kingdom of Vermont. Thanks to Bob Joly and the staff for inviting us to share the benefits of applying mindfulness with the community. Reeve Lindbergh, whose guidance in mindful journaling was an integral part of the course, has been a dear friend, valued advisor, and steadfast supporter for many years.

Thanks to the board of directors of Applied Mindfulness Training for their friendship and support. Also, much gratitude to the friends and family members who offered encouragement, financial support, and whatever else was needed to help keep AMT moving forward and me on track. Special thanks and appreciation to my son Andrew Hyman, who made time to read and offer astute observations on numerous iterations of the manuscript. Marie Hathaway, who manages communications for AMT, has been a persistent catalyst, an excellent editor and collaborator, and a steady believer in the value of this book. And a big thank you to Hazel Bercholz for her discerning design sense and enduring friendship.

Without the guidance of Chögyam Trungpa Rinpoche, I would not have known how to meet my own mind, much less help others do so. Finally, I realize that the person to whom I owe the most gratitude—for this book's existence and so much more—is my husband, Patton Hyman, the founder of Applied Mindfulness Training. He was my best friend and confidante for more than forty years and although he didn't live to see the finished product, he was the biggest champion of this work while it was in progress and I feel his support to this day. Love never dies.

60048960R00090

Made in the USA
Columbia, SC
11 June 2019